RENEWED LIFE
FOR SCOTTISH CASTLES

CBA Council for British Archaeology www.britarch.ac.uk

HISTORIC SCOTLAND ALBA AOSMHOR

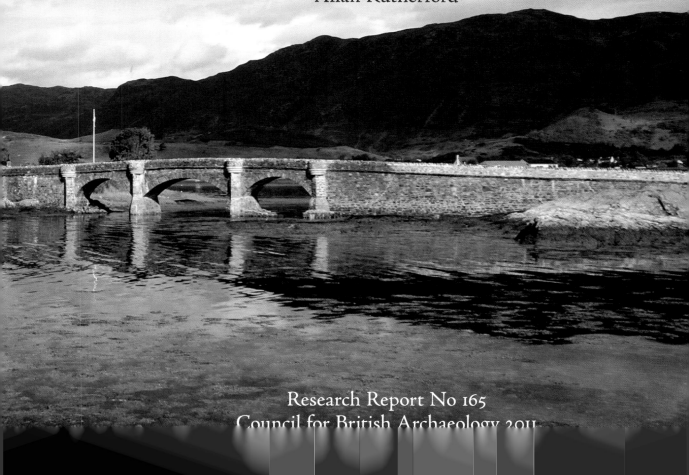

RENEWED LIFE
FOR
SCOTTISH CASTLES

Richard Fawcett
and
Allan Rutherford

Research Report No 165
Council for British Archaeology 2011

Published in 2011 by the Council for British Archaeology
St Mary's House, 66 Bootham, York, YO30 7BZ

British Library cataloguing in Publication Data
A catalogue record for this book is available from the British Library
ISBN 978-1-902771-86-1

Typeset by Carnegie Publishing Ltd
Printed and bound by Information Press, Oxford

The publisher acknowledges with gratitude a generous grant from Historic Scotland towards
the cost of publication

Frontispiece: Eilean Donan Castle (Dara Parsons)

Front cover: Aikwood Tower

Back cover: Dalquharran Old Castle; Stirling Castle, a barrack room in the Great Hall;
Tantallon Castle by Alexander Nasmyth

Contents

List of illustrations

Acknowledgements

The authors wish to offer their warmest thanks to a number of people for help of various kinds that has been offered in the course of writing this book. Amongst these are: Michelle Andersson, Iain Arnott, Luke Comins, Sean Conlon, Roger Curtis, Peter Drummond, Marc Ellington, Jamie Evans-Freke, Noel Fojut, Martyn and Penelope Gregory, Doreen Grove, David Henrie, Janet Hooper, John Jack, John Lewis, Lorna Main, John Malcolm, Raymond Morris, Stuart Morris, Tom Morton, Dara Parsons, Brian Paul, Mike Pendery, Krystyna Pytasz, Mike Rolland, John Sanders, Gordon Sleight, Gregor Stark, Lord and Lady Steel of Aikwood, Geoffrey Stell, Chris Tabraham, Benjamin Tindall, David Walker, Patricia Weeks, Andrew Wright, and Peter Yeoman.

Preface

There is a broad and persistent fascination with Scotland's castles and tower houses. This is reflected not only in the number of books and articles on the subject which are produced each year, but also in the very wide media interest, ranging from radio and television programmes on Scottish history through to tourism and property sales.

For those interested in this subject, one of the most long-running and at times heated debates in the media relates to castle restoration and reuse. Almost a century ago the acceptability of restoring ruins was the subject of detailed investigation by a joint House of Commons and House of Lords Select Committee, as part of agreeing the direction of heritage legislation that was subsequently adopted in 1913. Not surprisingly, Scottish witnesses gave strong views on the subject, including evidence from the then newly formed Royal Commission on the Ancient and Historical Monuments of Scotland and also from the architect Robert Rowand Anderson, who had been closely involved in works to restore several ruined Scottish buildings.

The questions remain relevant today in the castle and tower house context. Should the ruins be restored and brought back into use? If restoration is acceptable as a general principle, should all be restored or just some and, if the latter, how do we decide between possible candidates? In Scotland, recent debate has been focused around two cases, that of Castle Tioram on the Moidart Peninsula and that of Rowallan Castle in East Ayrshire. Each case has elicited strong views both for and against. Healthy debate is a very good thing, though on occasions this debate would have benefited from the wider availability of a range of information about castle and tower house restoration, its history, and its successes in Scotland.

In 2009, therefore, Historic Scotland took forward a new initiative involving Scottish castles and tower houses. The context for this was an earlier meeting hosted by Alex Salmond, Scotland's First Minister, and Linda Fabiani, the Minister for Europe, External Affairs and Culture, involving a range of experts who wished to improve understanding and release more potential for this key part of Scotland's historic environment. The First Minister proposed four closely linked projects to be taken forward by Historic Scotland on the Scottish government's behalf. The first was the creation of an online register describing a number of castles and tower houses that display qualities which might mean that restoration is in principle acceptable, subject to the identification of an appropriate scheme. The second was a best-practice guide for prospective restorers, drawing on the Scottish experience, and including a series of case studies and other resources. The third was the identification of an exemplary case study which could be used to develop wider public understanding and involvement. However, the timing of the economic downturn has meant that we have not yet identified a new project which could form this case study.

The final part of the initiative was to set out and publish an overview of the involvement of the state with castle restoration in Scotland, and that is the purpose of this volume. It is not, though, intended to present this history as a policy statement of Historic Scotland's current approach and philosophy, but rather to endeavour to set out the thinking of the state's advisers and of the owners and developers at particular times in the context of specific sites and specific projects. When confronted with a tower house which was restored, say, 30 or 50 years ago, it can be difficult to appreciate fully what approach to its restoration was adopted or why. However, there is much valuable information held on Historic Scotland's files which allows this story to be told, and this can be enhanced by information from, and discussions with, the restoring owners or their successors. This volume is not intended to be comprehensive but to provide a succinct overview, focusing on a number of key castles and tower houses in Scotland. There is far more information available than is included here but we hope that the volume will help to give background for the interested reader and to encourage their own researches.

The authors, Professor Richard Fawcett and Dr Allan Rutherford, are particularly well placed to write this volume. Richard's compendious knowledge of Scotland's architecture and archaeology has been developed first hand with Historic Scotland and its predecessors and he has had close involvement with a number of the sites described in this book. Allan brings his very broad experience of Scottish archaeology and architecture to bear, and he has a particular interest in Scottish castles and tower houses since they formed the basis of his doctoral thesis.

The story of castle and tower house restoration in Scotland is one of vision, optimism, determination, and fascination. We hope that this volume helps to tell this story.

Malcolm Cooper
Former Chief Inspector, Historic Scotland
July 2010

Section One
The Historical Background

CHAPTER I

The Scottish castle

Scotland is a nation in which castles figure prominently, both in the national consciousness and physically on the ground. Whether as buildings that continue to be occupied or as romantically evocative ruins, they draw large numbers of visitors from within Scotland itself and from around the world. Over recent centuries a significant number of people have chosen either to restore a Scottish castle for their own occupation or to carry out essential repairs in order to ensure that it can be passed on to future generations in a structurally stable condition. Most of the castles that have been worked on date from the period between the 15th and 17th centuries, when many were planned on a relatively modest scale that can lend itself surprisingly well to modern occupation, and that does not present an excessively daunting prospect for would-be restorers. In a high proportion of the earlier cases of castle restoration the people who undertook the work were either the owners of the estate on which the castle was situated, as at Dundas (West Lothian), or, as was the case at Duart (Argyll) (see Fig 3.2), they were the descendants of the builders and original occupants of the castle. By undertaking the restoration they were thus re-establishing both their connection with a building that was of the greatest importance for their family and that family's sense of its own history. During the last half-century, however, a growing number of individuals who have no direct historical connection with a particular building have been drawn to the idea of working on – and living in – a castle. There can be a wide range of motivations for doing this, but in the majority of cases a driving force has been quite simply that the aspiring restorer has fallen in love with the building, with its landscape setting, and with its history.

This small book aims to place castle restoration and conservation in Scotland within a broader context. Following a first chapter, in which a very brief outline history of Scottish castles is offered, in the next two chapters an attempt is made to provide an understanding of the attitudes that later occupants might have felt towards the castles of their ancestors, and the reasons why some of them chose to retain those castles at the heart of their residence. The second chapter also briefly explores how aesthetic attitudes towards castles developed in the course of the 18th century in particular, a period that is often referred to as the age of sensibility, and how ancient castles came to be seen as beautiful objects that could be an inspiration for artists, poets and intellectuals. In the third chapter a range of castles that were restored or conserved in the 19th and early 20th centuries is discussed. The main body of the book then consists of a number of more detailed case studies of projects that have been undertaken from around the mid-20th century onwards. In Chapter 23 there follows an outline of the role of the government in dealing with proposals for restoration at castles that have

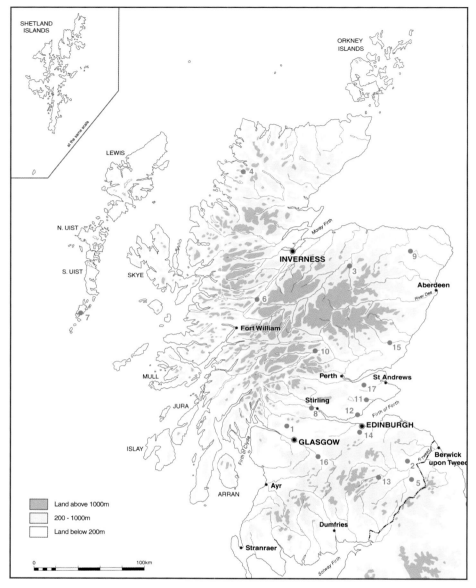

Figure 1.1 Map of places mentioned in Sections 2 and 3

1. Mugdock Castle
2. Hume Castle
3. Drumin Castle
4. Ardvreck Castle
5. Cessford Castle
6. Invergarry Castle
7. Kisimul Castle
8. Stirling Castle
9. Towie Barclay Castle
10. Castle Menzies
11. Balgonie Castle
12. Rossend Castle
13. Aikwood Tower
14. Liberton Tower
15. Melgund Castle
16. Hallbar Tower
17. Monimail, Cardinal Beaton's Tower

the statutory protection of scheduling or listing, and of how, on behalf of the government, Historic Scotland tries to ensure that the best possible outcome is achieved for both the castle and the restorer. Finally, in order to round off the picture, a retrospective view is offered by Professor David Walker, who was for many years head of the Inspectorate of Historic Buildings, and who was directly involved in a large number of cases of the grant-aided restoration of castles.

Here it should perhaps be noted that there is at the moment a healthy debate on how justifiable it is to refer to buildings of the kind that will be discussed in this book as 'castles'. Since so many of those that have lent themselves to restoration are very much more domestic than defensive in their planning and appearance, a number of people hold the view that to describe them as castles is inappropriate. However, castles always were designed to be both domestic and defensive in varying proportions, depending on the political and cultural climate of the times in which they were built, and the particular needs of the owners. Beyond that, documents dating from when they were constructed often use terms such as *castrum* (castle), *fortalicium* (fortress) and *turris* (tower), as well as the more domestic terms *manerium* (manor) and *domus* (house), so that the idea that their residence could be described as a castle would certainly not have appeared strange to their original occupants. Finally, since they are now almost universally referred to as castles, with little sense that they were designed for exclusively – or even predominantly – military functions, it seems unnecessary to abandon the use of such a widely accepted term in this context.

Those who wished to express their high status in the way that they lived, and had territories and possessions to protect if necessary, would always have designed their homes in ways that fulfilled both their domestic and defensive needs, and that made them stand out above the general run of dwellings. But the perception of medieval castles as places where the greater landholders lived in uncomfortably constrained conditions that were largely governed by military requirements is altogether misleading. In most cases there was an expectation that there would probably be relatively few occasions when a castle's defensibility would be put to the test: at the formidable castle of Tantallon (East Lothian) (see Fig 2.17), for example, only three sieges are known to have taken place over the 300 years of its active life. Thus, although an appearance of massive power might be an important part of the imagery that a great magnate wished to project at his principal residences, that certainly did not mean that handsome living quarters were not also provided, within which the most favoured members of the household could live in considerable luxury. This became even more the case from the 15th and 16th centuries. By then, the developing potential of gunpowder to break down all but the strongest walls meant that there were very few landowners who would be prepared to compromise the comfort in which they wished to live by making the daunting provisions that would have been necessary to defend themselves adequately against the possibility of an artillery attack. In any case, apart from the monarch, there were few who had the resources to acquire and maintain the very expensive guns and ammunition necessary for an artillery attack. An appearance of defensibility tended to remain part of the essential vocabulary of a great house, with a number of gunloops frequently supplementing or replacing wall-head crenellations as the most prominent expression of that defensibility. But, while it was probably wise to be able to close one's doors firmly against those one had offended if the need arose, by that stage the prestige and comfort of the house's principal occupants tended to be even more of a primary consideration than before.

The earliest medieval castles have left rather misleading evidence of themselves. For many, perhaps the majority, the principal building materials were timber and earth, and all that now remains of them is the eroded earthwork substructures. Within those earthworks limited evidence for the structures they supported may have survived to some extent, and that evidence has occasionally been explored archaeologically, with fascinating results. The earthworks themselves, however, usually appear as little more than circular or rectangular arrangements of earth mounds and ditches, sometimes known as ringworks, or as taller hemispherical or conical mounds, usually referred to as mottes. The linear mounds of the ringworks once provided a base for the defensive palisades and ditches of enclosures, within which would have been a number of timber buildings, while on the mottes a tower or hall would usually have been located. The two forms were often combined to form what is known as a motte and bailey, one of the best preserved examples of which is to be seen at the Bass of Inverurie (Aberdeenshire) (Fig 1.2).

From what we now see of these castles, they might appear to have been very simple in form and rather basic in their provisions. It must be remembered, however, that even great royal castles were generally largely of timber and earth in their earliest forms, and when the timber had been covered with a relatively thick lime-based coating, the appearance may have been little different from that of a masonry building, where the stone work would have been similarly concealed beneath a lime render. It should also be borne in mind that timber castles continued to be built for longer than is generally assumed. In the 1320s the buildings within Robert I's much loved residence at his *manerium* of Cardross (Dunbartonshire), for example, appear to have been at least partly of timber. Even in castles that eventually came to be predominantly built of stone, timber may have continued to be a principal building material until later than is commonly thought, as was perhaps the case at Huntly (Aberdeenshire), while in other cases stone residences may have sheltered behind timber defensive lines, as at the Doune of Invernochty (Aberdeenshire). Timber also remained in use for some of the lesser buildings, and for subdivisions within the main buildings, especially in the more extensively compartmented upper floors. As late as 1424, when the castle at Linlithgow (West Lothian) was destroyed by fire, many of the buildings presumably incorporated a great deal of timber since it burned so readily.

Figure 1.2 The Bass of Inverurie, the earthworks of the motte and bailey

RENEWED LIFE FOR SCOTTISH CASTLES

Figure 1.3
Dunstaffnage Castle
(© Crown copyright)

Nevertheless, by the later 12th and 13th centuries, growing numbers of the more ambitious castles were being built largely of stone. The principal masonry element of those castles tended to be a robustly constructed curtain wall around the main enclosure, which in some cases followed the outline of a rock outcrop that had been selected for both its visual prominence and its greater defensibility. Several castles of this kind are to be seen in the west of Scotland, as at Dunstaffnage (Argyll) (Fig 1.3), though there were probably also more in the Lowland regions before Robert I ordered several to be destroyed so that they could not be held against him. Hume (Berwickshire) appears to have been one example in the area of the Borders (see Figs 6.1–6.2). Major royal castles such as those at Edinburgh and Stirling (see Fig 13.2), which are perched high on volcanic rocks, were also essentially of this type, though on a much greater scale, and, apart from a delightful small chapel at Edinburgh (see Fig 3.6), nothing that is now seen at either is earlier than the end of the 14th century.

Where there was no need to respond to geological features, the plan might be closer to a regular square or rectangle, as at Castle Sween (Argyll) or Lochindorb (Nairn), though it might be a circle, as at Rothesay (Bute) (see Fig 3.9). In many of these cases the buildings within the curtain wall would have been in the form of lean-to ranges against the interior of the walls, and at first would often have been of timber, which usually means that few traces remain other than joist or rafter pockets along the walls. By the 13th century, the curtain walls were increasingly supplemented by rectangular or round towers at the angles, sometimes with particular emphasis given to a great gatehouse that might be symmetrically flanked by a pair of such towers, as at Caerlaverock (Dumfriesshire) (Fig 1.4). Towers of these kinds, which perhaps ultimately looked back to Roman examples, had considerable defensive advantages, in the way that they strengthened the walls and allowed for defensive fire along the outer face of the walls. But they also made the castles to which they were attached enormously impressive, and there can be little doubt that the array of towers planned for, but only partly built, at Bothwell (Lanarkshire) was intended to make plain to those who beheld them

Figure 1.4
Caerlaverock Castle,
the gatehouse
(© Crown copyright)

that the principal occupant was a person of great consequence and military might.

By this stage, ideas on the accommodation required in an aristocratic residence were becoming more fixed. In documents across Europe the principal spaces required begin to be referred to as *aula*, *camera* and *capella*, that is hall, chamber and chapel. At Robert I's manor of Cardross the main accommodation consisted of the hall, the queen's chamber, the chapel, the kitchen and the larder, and a new chamber was added slightly later. Except in the most ambitious Scottish castles, the space set aside for the chapel is not always clearly identifiable, and it may often have been little more than an oratory in a window recess of the principal chamber, as was the case at Loch Leven (Kinross-shire) (Fig 1.5). The hall and chamber are usually identifiable if enough of the buildings have survived, and in some cases there was more than one of each. The hall was essentially the most public space of the castle, where the owner, his wider household and guests might come together when appropriate, and where the owner would carry out some of his administrative, judicial and ceremonial functions. In the great royal castles and palaces, by the end of the Middle Ages the hall was generally an enormously impressive building that was intended to symbolise the king's supreme authority, as is seen most notably at Stirling and Edinburgh.

As the years passed, there was a tendency for the owner to seek more privacy for himself and his immediate household, and in the greater castles he increasingly chose to have a separate hall that was in effect the outermost part of a suite of rooms that could be described as a lodging, sometimes in addition to a more widely accessible great hall. Beyond this hall would have been his chamber, which was initially both his bedroom and living room, though later those functions could be divided between an outer and an inner chamber, each of which may have been provided with more intimate spaces known as closets. Lodgings of this kind in Scotland appear to have been sometimes referred to as *palatia*, which can be translated as 'palace', although usually without any intention of conveying the sense of architectural magnificence that is now associated with that word. By the later 14th century, all of these rooms are likely to have had fireplaces and latrines, and could be made very comfortable when furnished, upholstered and hung with fabrics. In addition to these principal rooms there would have been a need for kitchens, larders, sculleries and beer and wine cellars to serve the owner's culinary needs, and there would also have been stables, byres and a wide range of agricultural and storage facilities either within the main castle enclosure or spread around one or more outer courtyards.

Figure 1.5 Loch Leven Castle, the oratory in a window embrasure of the tower chamber

The principal accommodation within castles of this kind could thus be very much more comfortable than the ruined appearance of so many of them might now suggest. However, in some of the larger castles the accommodation may be more extensive than would be suitable for the needs of most modern families, since they were designed to accommodate great households. Alternatively, some may be so small and inward looking that life within them would be rather constrained for all but the most determined castle restorer. Where castles of the latter kind have been restored for occupation, the resultant accommodation may not be especially easy to live in, as has been the case at Kisimul (Barra), for example (see Figs 12.1–12.3).

An owner's personal lodging within a castle could be designed in a variety of ways. Initially, it was often a series of separate structures that might adjoin each other or be connected by corridors, and that might be either at ground level or increasingly commonly raised to first-floor height above a basement. There are a number of examples of first-floor halls that are of very striking appearance, such as that at Rait (Nairn) of a date around

1300 (Fig 1.6). In the grandest castles, however, the owner's lodging was often within a tower that was given particular individual prominence, as in the circular example at Bothwell (Lanarkshire) of the late 13th century, or in one of a number of towers around the perimeter of the castle, as with the rectangular examples at Mugdock (Stirlingshire) of the later 14th century (see Figs 5.1–5.4).

In later medieval Scotland, in common with a number of other parts of Europe, growing numbers of castles began to have their principal lodging within a single purpose-built tower-like building that is usually referred to as a tower house. These could vary widely in scale, from that at the great episcopal residence of Spynie (Moray) to the very much smaller tower of the Moultray family on a coastal rock promontory at Seafield (Fife). The Scottish examples generally had a basement for storage, a first-floor hall (where the entrance was often located in the earlier examples), and one or more chambers on the upper floors, all linked by a spiral stair at one corner. There was usually a barrel vault over at least the basement, and possibly over other floors as well; such vaults had the advantage that they both strengthened the structure and provided some protection against fire. The date at which these tower houses first began to be built is uncertain; although it has been suggested that some could be as early as the 13th century, including that at Drum (Aberdeenshire) (Fig 1.7), such an early date is open to doubt. In fact few of the earlier tower houses are likely to date from before the later 14th century, a period when castle building gathered fresh momentum after the wearisomely long wars with England, and they continued to be built through the 15th and 16th centuries. Buildings of this kind received what might be thought of as a royal seal of approval when David II started one for himself in Edinburgh Castle in about 1368. Tower houses were to prove remarkably versatile, and already at Edinburgh there was an offshoot in the form of a small wing at one

Figure 1.6 Rait Castle

Figure 1.7 Drum Castle, the tower house

corner. In later towers such wings often contained smaller chambers than those in the main block, and, since those smaller chambers might have lower ceilings than the rooms in the main block, there could also be more floors in the wing. In a tower that Robert II built for himself on his family estates at Dundonald (Ayrshire) (Fig 1.8), after he succeeded to the throne in 1371, the plan was considerably more elongated than was usual. The principal hall or chamber was evidently on the top floor, where it was covered by a handsome ribbed vault, and from where there were splendid views across the surrounding countryside. In this it can perhaps be seen as a fusion of the more elongated plan seen at two-storeyed hall houses such as Rait (see Fig 1.6), and the newly emerging preference for something of more tower-like form. Extraordinary ingenuity was to be displayed in the planning of tower houses, resulting in a range of L-shaped and Z-shaped plans. More complex variants are to be seen in a U-shaped plan at Borthwick (Midlothian) and a cross-shaped plan at Denmylne (Fife) (Fig 1.9), while at Crookston (Renfrewshire) a rectangular main tower had smaller square towers projecting from all four angles.

There is such variety in the range of forms that some commentators have understandably suggested that the single modern blanket term 'tower house' loses any validity. However, it is important to understand that, while these buildings can hardly ever have been intended to stand in isolation, as the element within which the owner's own lodging was accommodated, they were probably always meant to derive particular prominence from their height and more architecturally impressive form. The tower was a potent symbol in the medieval mind, as is clear from many literary sources. Thus, while the term tower house is perhaps not strictly accurate as a description used to cover all of the very large numbers of tower-like lordly or lairdly houses built in the centuries on each side of the Reformation, it does usefully express a likely aspect of the aspirations of their builders.

The provision of buildings in addition to a tower house within a castle depended on the wealth, social standing and aspirations of the owner. For a small landowner, there might be a requirement for nothing more than a few buildings set around the edges of a single small courtyard to meet his administrative,

domestic and agricultural needs. Many of the greater magnates, however, would have needed very much more than that, and the visual impact of the tower house might be at least partly lessened as it came to be subsumed within a series of courtyards surrounded by ancillary buildings of considerable scale. In addition to all of the functions that had to be housed at the principal residences of a major landholder, there would be gardens, intended to be both areas for recreational resort and places where produce for the owner's table could be cultivated. By the 16th century, if not before, these gardens might be contained within walls that sheltered the plants from the harsh northern winds, or they might be set out on a series of southward-facing terraces; both kinds are still to be seen at Aberdour (Fife), for example. Edzell (Angus) has one of the most extraordinary walled gardens in Britain (Fig 1.10). Dating from 1604, it has richly sculpted decoration on classical themes around the walls, together with nesting boxes for song birds, and a banqueting house and bath house at its outer corners. On a summer's day it would have offered an altogether delightful feast for both the senses and the intellect.

Tower houses continued to be built as the principal structure of many castles over a long period, presumably largely because they were seen as being architecturally impressive, while their scale could be readily adapted to their owner's needs and the depth of his purse. As will be discussed in the next chapter, the continuing cachet that they were evidently deemed to give to a castle and its owner is also evident in the large numbers that were retained at the heart of the owner's residence, even after they had ceased to serve their original purpose. One reason why they might cease to serve their original function was that, while many later tower houses were certainly planned on a very generous scale, there were limitations on living in even the largest of them. These limitations stemmed chiefly from the virtual impossibility of modifying room sizes, from the restrictions of lighting through relatively small windows set in thick walls, and from the inconvenience of access between floors by means of a usually quite narrow spiral stair. Some of these limitations could be mitigated if there was the will and the means, as at Rosyth (Fife), where the hall was enlarged by the laborious process of paring back the end walls, and by cutting great new windows through the reduced thickness of those walls. But such solutions were not easy to achieve, and from as early as the central decades of the 15th century some owners preferred to provide themselves with more spacious lodgings of a hall and chamber that were set out horizontally, usually at first-floor level above a series of vaulted chambers, and that could be approached by a more impressively spacious stair.

In such cases the earlier tower house was generally retained as a prestigious architectural feature, even though it no longer served as the castle's principal residence. The later 15th and earlier 16th centuries were to see large numbers of such ranges of lodgings being added to tower houses, from Dean (Ayrshire) in the west (Fig 1.11) to Balgonie (Fife) in the east (see Figs 16.1–16.3). But, as was

Figure 1.10 Edzell Castle, the tower house and garden (© Crown copyright)

Figure 1.11 Dean Castle

often the case, royal precedents were important in giving greater popularity to the fashion for horizontally extended lodgings, and the residence that was built in the 1490s for James IV on the highest point of the rock of Stirling Castle, on the opposite side of the principal square from his magnificent new great hall, was probably highly influential in this (see Figs 13.1–13.6). It had a hall, a great chamber and a chamber, as well as a small kitchen and a number of lesser rooms. It was immediately copied at Castle Campbell (Clackmannanshire), albeit on a more compressed scale than that at Stirling.

This was only the beginning of a more expansive phase of domestic planning in the houses of the wealthier landholders, however. From the mid-16th century, there was a growing requirement for adequate space both to accommodate great households, which would have included some individuals who were themselves of high birth, and to give architectural expression to the standing and taste of the owner. To meet these needs, additional chambers and lodgings were often provided. There might also be galleries that connected the rooms and afforded an enclosed area for exercise at times of inclement weather, and that might be the place where the owner's family portraits and objects of *vertu* were displayed to best advantage. In some cases, all of this might be contained within buildings added around the periphery of a pre-existing principal courtyard. As a result of such progressive additions and periodic remodelling, the residual open space within the courtyard might be greatly reduced, as was the case at Crichton (Midlothian)

Figure 1.12 Crichton Castle, the courtyard
(© Crown copyright)

Figure 1.13 Tolquhon Castle, the courtyard

(Fig 1.12), or Caerlaverock (Dumfriesshire). In other cases the courtyard might be treated as a more open space from within which the qualities of the surrounding buildings could be easily admired by those permitted access, as at Tolquhon (Aberdeenshire) (Fig 1.13) or Edzell (Angus) (Fig 1.10).

This concludes our brief overview of castle design, and we can now move on to consider how later generations responded to the castles.

CHAPTER 2

Attitudes to castles up to the mid-19th century

Earlier attitudes towards the preservation of ancestral residences in Scotland

It is always dangerous to attempt generalisations about presumed national attitudes when one is looking to the relatively distant past, and especially when the evidence is very incomplete. But in the early modern period it does appear to be the case that a significant proportion of Scottish landholders continued to see in the castellated houses of their ancestors a highly potent expression of their own proud lineage and dignity. In parallel with this, it seems that those who had recently risen in status and acquired estates might often value the existing house that came with the lands as one of the means by which they could place the stamp of authority on their new social standing. This certainly did not prevent many of those who could afford to do so from adding more convenient and commodious residential quarters to those historic houses, in response to changing architectural fashions and rising aspirations for domestic comfort. Nevertheless, even the most cursory glance through the pages of MacGibbon and Ross's *Castellated and domestic architecture of Scotland* makes clear that large numbers of later residences retained parts of an earlier castle within the extended complex, and very often in a highly visible manner.

It cannot be ruled out that, where parts of a castle were retained within later buildings, economy might be a factor. The temptation to dismiss the majority of retentions simply as evidence of parsimony, however, is dispelled when it is realised that those retained parts might be of relatively limited use in the expanded domestic arrangements. Beyond that, the way in which an earlier tower was so frequently prominently located within enlarged houses of the 16th and 17th centuries, and in a way that presented it as one of the first features to be seen on the main approach to the house, suggests that its retention was a matter of some significance. At a castle such as Edzell (Angus) (see Fig 2.1), which was extended in the mid- and late 16th century for the Lindsay family, the existing tower was given a place at one end of a new entrance front, with a circular tower at the other end of the front to emphasise further the castellated imagery of the buildings. A similar approach was taken, amongst many other cases, at the Forbes family's castle at Tolquhon (Aberdeenshire), where the new work was carried out in the 1580s, and where a gatehouse that imitated on a diminutive scale the great

Figure 2.1 Edzell
Castle, the entrance
front

twin-towered gatehouses of the 13th century gave prominence to the entrance. At
Edzell the importance of the tower was further emphasised when it became the
visually dominant element on the edge of the wonderful new garden created in
1604 (see Fig 1.10).

Edzell and Tolquhon have long passed out of use. The Lindsays were forced
to sell their estate at the former in 1715, and it was eventually stripped out in
1764, while the Forbes family sold its estate in 1716, though parts of the castle
continued in reduced occupation until around the middle of the 19th century.
In many other cases of this type, however, the whole complex has continued in
occupation until the present, or at least until relatively recent times. At Drum
Castle (Aberdeenshire) the starting point for later developments was an imposing
tower that, as has been seen, is considered by some to be as early as the 13th
century (see Fig 1.7). This was augmented in 1619 by a new range that may itself
incorporate parts of the medieval buildings that would have been progressively
added within the confines of the walled enclosures around the tower. At Drum
the whole house continued in occupation by the Irvine family until as late as 1975,
with periodic changes being carried out until then, including the installation of a
library within the tower in the 1840s.

The number of major Scottish houses in which parts of an earlier castellated
residence of some kind has been retained suggests that many of his contemporaries
would have agreed with Sir Robert Kerr in 1632 when he advised: 'by any means
do not take away the battlement … for that is the grace of the house, and makes
it look like a castle, and hence so noblest …'.

It was presumably similar attitudes which meant that, around the time of his
Scottish homecoming in 1633, Charles I contemplated building at his palace of
Holyrood a turreted chamber tower balancing that built by James V in 1528–32,
in order to create a symmetrical castle-like arrangement across its entrance front.

Figure 2.2 The Palace of Holyrood, the entrance front

That is itself of considerable interest, since Charles's personal architectural tastes appear to have inclined more towards a highly refined variant of classicism. The construction of the pendant tower did not prove possible at that time, and it was not until the 1670s that the proposal was put into effect for Charles II (Fig 2.2). It was presumably on the advice of the Duke of Lauderdale that this was done, however, and not because of any expressed wish by Charles II, who had little love for his northern kingdom. In a similar spirit to that displayed at Holyrood, in the 1680s the Earl of Kinghorne and Strathmore chose to emphasise the appearance of antiquity of his castle at Glamis (Angus), taking his lead from an earlier remodelling of 1606–20 in the course of the works that he carried out (Fig 2.3). This was despite a slightly puzzling statement by the earl in 1684 that 'there is no man more against these old fashion of tours and castles than I am'.

Figure 2.3 Glamis Castle

There were, of course, many cases where factors militated against the continued occupation of castellated houses. Amongst such considerations were the acquisition or inheritance of a finer or more conveniently located house elsewhere, or a decline in status by the owning family, with the consequent inability either to expand or to maintain their house to the necessary standard. At Balvaird (Perthshire), a fine tower built around 1500 for a branch of the Murray family was no longer of use as a primary residence when the centre of that family's expanded estates shifted to the mellower lands of Scone. Yet, while the less substantially built ancillary buildings ranged around a series of courtyards at

Balvaird were consequently allowed to fall into decay, the more robust principal tower continued to stand, and in the later 19th century it was reroofed to serve as accommodation for estate workers. In that case the fact that the barony of Balvaird was one of the titles of the Earls of Mansfield could have been a consideration behind the reluctance to allow the tower to collapse.

In some cases a family's circumstances meant that a tower and associated buildings that were of relatively slight pretensions, even when first built, hardly expanded beyond those initial aspirations throughout the course of their history of occupation. At Buckholm (Roxburghshire) a modest courtyard of buildings with an L-plan tower at one corner, which is thought to have been started for John Pringle in 1582, continued to be partly occupied into the 18th century with periodic relatively minor augmentations and modifications (Fig 2.4). While it was probably never more than a lesser laird's residence and working farm, it was of a scale that allowed it to continue in use over a long period for purposes similar to those for which it was originally built. It ceased to be a primary residence when it passed to a branch of the family that was based at Torwoodlee, around the mid-18th century, though a modest new farmhouse was built for tenants next to the old tower, and that house continued in occupation into the early 20th century. Later use by individuals of a lower social status than those for whom a castle was built, as at Balvaird and Buckholm, was to be a relatively common reason for their being at least partly retained. Nevertheless, many castles did continue to be occupied by, and modified for, later generations of the families that had built or subsequently acquired them, with the most architecturally prominent parts of the complex often carefully preserved.

Figure 2.4 Buckholm Tower

The ways in which a continuing value might be placed on earlier work by later owners is demonstrated at many multi-period houses. Since the mid-16th century, Balbegno (Kincardineshire) has had as its chief focus an impressive tower built by John Wood in 1569; amongst its most notable features are a splendid quadripartite vault over the hall and delightful relief carvings at the wall head. This tower clearly continued to be valued by the later owners of the estate, a branch of the Ogilvy family, since they retained it while adding a relatively small-scale range to one side in the 18th century as their residential quarters. As at Drum, there must be a suspicion that the 18th-century range was on the site of – and perhaps even embodied – buildings closer in date to the tower, but in this case the new work is dwarfed by the old, and visually subservient to it. The contrast between old and new is just as clear, albeit in a different way, at Touch (Stirlingshire). In full view to one side of a very handsome seven-bay pedimented house of around 1750, which was built for a branch of the Seton family by Gideon Gray, there projects a small battlemented 16th-century tower, and further inspection reveals that the rear part of the house is entirely earlier work. Unlike at Balbegno, the new work is given greater architectural weight than the old, but it is the way that the tower was left projecting to one side of the smart new front that suggests the contrast between old and new was not simply tolerated but was relished.

Around the time that Touch was under construction, at a number of houses it began to be seen as a possibility that an ancestral home might set the tone for the entire architectural idiom of new work, at least so far as the exterior was concerned. A prestigious precedent for the revival of towered and castellated exteriors was established at the Duke of Argyll's castle of Inveraray (Argyll),

Figure 2.5 Inveraray Castle

Figure 2.6 Robert
Adam, *Landscape
with a castle* (courtesy
of the National
Gallery of Scotland)

which was started in 1745 to the designs of Roger Morris (Fig 2.5). There had
been an extended period of gestation before then, however, with the gentleman-
architect Sir John Vanbrugh, who had already built a house in the form of a castle
for himself at Greenwich, producing a castellated design as early as the 1720s.
At Inveraray the decision was taken to build the new house on a site adjacent
to the family's ancestral tower; but, unlike the cases we have so far considered,
that tower was then demolished. In this case an old castle was being entirely
superseded by a new one, although the retention of a castellated image was
clearly of the highest importance for the duke, a great territorial magnate in both
Highland and Lowland Scotland.

The architect who was to make the greatest contribution to an early taste for
newly constructed castellated houses in Scotland was Robert Adam. Despite
being in the vanguard of a fresh wave of highly refined Neoclassicism, Adam was
an admirer of medieval castles, and also, incidentally, of the sense of movement
that he perceived in Vanbrugh's architecture. One of the directions in which his
extraordinarily fertile imagination extended is seen in his sketches of fantastic
multi-towered castles set in wild landscapes, which reveal a strikingly Romantic
spirit that seems far removed from the opulent elegance of so many of the
drawing rooms he designed (Fig 2.6). Indeed, some of those sketches could well
have served as illustrations for *The Castle of Otranto*. That prototype Gothic
novel, published in 1764, was the product of the slightly fevered imagination of
Horace Walpole, who had started to build a house for himself in a variety of
medieval styles at Strawberry Hill in Twickenham in the 1750s, and together the

novel and the house are significant indicators of an important developing strand in the intellectual climate of the times. Fortunately for Adam, a number of his Scottish – and some English – patrons were themselves sufficiently in tune with these ideas to allow him to give them tangible external form in the new residences they commissioned from him. As at Inveraray, the owners of most of these externally medieval-style houses were looking for something more gracious internally; however, in some cases, as at the Duke of Northumberland's Alnwick Castle, Adam was also given scope to design delicately detailed Gothic interiors.

Adam was sufficiently responsive to the spirit of the places in which he worked to be able to take a wide range of approaches in his dealings with castles. In an abortive proposal of 1774 at Barnbougle (Midlothian) the remodelled old tower was to have been at the apex of a highly imaginative triangular composition, which clearly expressed Adam's love of movement. A different approach was taken at Dalquharran (Ayrshire), where the decision was reached to preserve the old castle as a ruined eye-catcher in the landscape (Fig 2.7) as viewed from the castellated house that was built higher up the hillside in 1782–90 (Fig 2.8). In those two cases, the roles of the existing castles, although widely differing, were clearly major conditioning factors in what was proposed. But at what was eventually to be Adam's most sublime castellated composition, the Earl of Cassilis's Culzean Castle (Ayrshire), the old tower was completely subsumed and hidden between two new wings (Fig 2.9). That was done in a first building phase carried out between 1777 and 1781, and it almost seems as if it was deemed sufficient to know that the adopted castellated architectural forms were sanctioned by what lay hidden within them. In a second phase, between 1787 and 1792, an altogether more monumentally modelled range, with a massive axial drum tower, was added on the very edge of the cliff (Fig 2.10). There it soars above the wave-swept shore in a way that must have thrilled

Figure 2.7
Dalquharran Old
Castle

Figure 2.8
Dalquharran New
Castle

Figure 2.9 Culzean Castle, the garden front

Figure 2.10 Culzean Castle, the front towards the sea

many a romantic young maiden's heart as she gazed out from the classical security of the drawing room, or as she dreamed of the corsair who might carry her away while her maid dressed her hair before dinner.

The beautiful, the picturesque and the sublime

By the time that Adam was at work on these houses, intellectual attitudes within Europe as a whole had become coloured by the development of aesthetic philosophies in which landscapes, and the buildings within them, tended to be classified into the categories of 'beautiful', 'picturesque' and 'sublime'. The landscapes of Scotland were generally deemed to fall more frequently into the two latter categories. Although ideas on the sublime had their roots in the 17th century, the concept was to be defined most precisely in Edmund Burke's *Philosophical enquiry into our ideas of the sublime and beautiful*, published in 1757. There he described how, for a prospect to be truly sublime, the individual had to feel himself subject to the largely uncontrollable forces of nature, with a resultant sense of awe and even of terror.

The inevitable decay of everything that human endeavour might achieve, which was central to the idea of the sublime, was seen as being particularly poignantly expressed in the ruins of great buildings, especially when nature was found to be inexorably re-establishing its hold through the growth of vegetation over the collapsing masonry. There is a frisson of delicious alarm in the way that the English poet Thomas Gray (1716–71) describes how:

... from that yonder ivy-mantled tow'r,
The moping owl does to the moon complain.

Similar themes continued to be explored in the poetry of such as Hartley
Coleridge (1796–1849), as in his question:

Hast thou not seen an age rifted tower
Meet habitation for the Ghost of Time
Where fearful ravage makes decay sublime
And destitution wears the face of power?

In a specifically Scottish context, in 1797 a namesake of Robert Burns was
inspired by the ruins of Cadzow Castle (Lanarkshire) (Fig 2.11) to write two
poems in which the favoured themes were again rehearsed. In one he urged:

Passing stranger ponder here,
Grandeur's ruins claim a tear
View in me thy coming fate.

Having taken the castle as a reminder of human mortality in one poem, in the
second he toyed with both its cladding of ivy and its ghostly qualities:

Thou ruined castle ivy-bound
Where storied ghosts terrific cry.

Many authors continued to be enchanted by the supernatural aspects of ruins,
and the sense of foreboding evoked in the description of the light in Sir Walter

Figure 2.11 Cadzow
Castle (© Crown
copyright)

RENEWED LIFE FOR SCOTTISH CASTLES

Scott's *Rosabelle* is especially effective because of the fact that it was over the castles of Roslin (see Fig 2.15) and Hawthornden (see Fig 2.16) that it played:

It glar'd on Roslin's castled rock,
　It ruddied all the copse-wood glen;
'Twas seen from Dryden's groves of ash
　And seen from cavern'd Hawthornden.

There was, of course, at the same time an element of *schadenfreude* in the realisation that even the buildings of the mighty were so evidently doomed to decay in due course, as expressed by John Dyer (1700–55) in his *Grongar Hill*:

A little rule, a little sway
A sunbeam in a winter's day
Is all the proud and mighty have
Between the cradle and the grave.

A sense of the inevitability of death and the melancholic contemplation of the mutability of all human creation can be strangely comforting, and happy indeed were most landowners who had a handsomely composed ruin within the sight-lines of their house to remind them of this. While the resolutely sensible Duchess of Marlborough had been resistant to Sir John Vanbrugh's pleadings to retain the ruins of Woodstock Manor in the landscape of Blenheim Palace in 1709, in *c* 1686 Sir William Bruce had decided to position the precociously classical house he was planning for himself at Kinross so that the main vista was aligned on the island where the ruins of Loch Leven Castle (Kinross-shire) stood (Fig 2.12). Loch Leven had the additional cachet of its association with the imprisonment and escape of the tragic Mary Queen of Scots. The value of a ruined castle within a gentleman's park was clearly stated by Richard Payne Knight, a leading aesthetic theoretician of the later 18th century, in his poem of 1794, *The landscape, a didactic poem*:

Bless'd too is he, who midst his tufted trees
Some ruin'd castle's lofty tower sees;
Imbosom'd high upon the mountain's brow,
Or nodding o'er the stream that glides below.

Where an existing castellated ruin could not be brought into service as a view-stopper, a new one might be raised. The Hundy Mundy built at Mellerstain (Berwickshire) in 1726 for George Baillie, and The Whim at Blair Castle (Perthshire), built for the Duke of Atholl in 1762 (Fig 2.13), were examples of this approach. In those cases, however, the results were little more than two-dimensional silhouettes meant to be seen at a distance. By contrast, at the Earl of Breadalbane's Taymouth Castle (Perthshire) eye-catchers known as the Tower and the Fort, both of which are thought to date from *c* 1765, are more substantially three-dimensional, and this was to be true of most later structures of the kind.

Figure 2.12 Loch
Leven Castle as seen
from Kinross House

In comparison with what underlay the appreciation of the sublime, the cult of
the picturesque fostered rather less dramatic attitudes, in which the aim was to
see how landscapes might reflect the works of painters such as Claude Lorrain
(Fig 2.14) and Nicolas Poussin. A certain degree of roughness was still valued,
in which artfully disposed ruins, preferably framed by trees rising amidst moss-
covered rocks, were a highly appreciated element. Yet the proponents of the
picturesque, while revealing rather quarrelsome tendencies in deciding just what
it was that they sought, did not wish to be as overwhelmed by their experience
as did those who were in search of the sublime. Before the later 18th century the
Highlands of Scotland had tended to be viewed with dismay, as is evident from
the description of Lochaber in Daniel Defoe's *A tour thro' the whole island of Great
Britain* of 1724–26:

> It is indeed a frightful country full of hideous desart mountains and
> unpassable, except to the Highlanders who possess the precipices.
> Here in spight of the most vigorous pursuit, the Highland robbers,

Figure 2.13 Blair
Castle, the castellated
eye-catcher known as
The Whim

such as the famous Rob Roy in the late disturbances, find such retreats as none can pretend to follow them into, nor could he be ever taken.

This fear of desolation was to change. The Revd William Gilpin, who began a series of tours in search of picturesque scenes in 1769, eventually reached Scotland in 1776, and in 1789 published the two volumes of his *Observations relative chiefly to Picturesque Beauty, made in the year 1776, on several parts of Great Britain; particularly the High-Lands of Scotland*. Gilpin himself appears to have been rather challenged by the Scottish landscape because, apart from other considerations, much of what he saw was insufficiently wooded to fit in with his ideas of what was acceptably picturesque, and at least one vista that was generally held to be fine was dismissed by him as 'not indeed picturesque'. Nevertheless, growing numbers of visitors came to visit Scotland for the qualities of its scenery, and a number of castles were soon regarded as obligatory stations on their route. Amongst these were pre-eminently Roslin (Midlothian) (Fig 2.15) and Hawthornden (Midlothian) (Fig 2.16) but others, including Edinburgh, Stirling, Corra (on the Falls of the Clyde) and Bothwell (Lanarkshire), were added to a growing list.

Figure 2.14 A pastoral landscape by Claude Lorrain 1645 (Claude Gellee, 1600–82) (© The Barber Institute of Fine Arts, University of Birmingham/ the Bridgeman Art Library)

Figure 2.15 Roslin Castle, as depicted by Paul Sandby *c* 1780 (courtesy of the Yale Centre for British Art, Paul Mellon Collection, B1975.4.1877)

Figure 2.16 Hawthornden Castle, as depicted by Francis Grose in 1789

It was expected of those who published accounts of their trips to Scotland that they would carefully point out the picturesque scenes they encountered for the benefit of those who came after. Thomas Pennant, who made his second tour of Scotland in 1772 and published his account of it two years later, could be a little terse in this regard, as in his reference to Borthwick Castle (Midlothian), despite the fact that it apparently scored all the necessary points: 'About a mile farther is Borthwick castle, seated on a knowl in the midst of a pretty vale, bounded by hills covered with corn and woods; a most picturesque scene'.

Francis Grose, in the two volumes of his *Antiquities of Scotland*, published in 1789–91, was inclined to be more fulsome, as in his description of Hawthornden:

> From the window of these buildings, as well as from the adjacent garden, there is a most delightful and romantic prospect, similar to those given by poets of Fairy land, the river Esk running with a murmuring stream close under the eye, through a deep rocky glen, whose sides are clothed with wood to the water's edge, the stream here and there breaking against large stones, or the projecting rocks, which exhibit a variety of picturesque forms tinged with different colours. What greatly adds to the beauty of the scene is, that though the banks are plentifully wooded, there are here and there bare spots through which the rocks contrasted with the foliage appear to great advantage … Roslin and Hawthornden make two of the fashionable excursions for all strangers visiting Edinburgh. Indeed those who have not seen them, particularly the latter, have missed some of the most beautiful and picturesque scenes in the south of Scotland.

Grose included a high proportion of views of castles in the illustrations to his volumes, in which their picturesque and beautiful qualities are meant to be clear

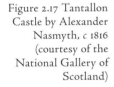

Figure 2.17 Tantallon Castle by Alexander Nasmyth, *c* 1816 (courtesy of the National Gallery of Scotland)

(see Figs 2.16 and 6.2), and by this stage growing numbers of artists were already being drawn to Scotland's castles as a focus for their art. Following the defeat of the Jacobites at Culloden in 1746, the young Paul Sandby had been part of a team sent north from England to record potential barracks and defensible castles in the Highlands. But, whilst carefully recording a number of the castles of the western seaboard for this purpose, his views of such as Tioram (Inverness-shire) and Duart (Argyll) leave little doubt of the warmth of his response to these buildings within their landscape – and seascape – settings. He was also at pains to visit other castles, including a number on the usual picturesque circuit, and his view of Roslin is especially delightful (see Fig 2.15). The memory of some castles was to remain with him, as may be seen from a series of views of Bothwell Castle that he painted many years after he had returned to England.

This is not the place to offer more than the briefest account of the stimulus that has been offered to artists by Scotland's castles in the course of the later 18th and 19th centuries. But amongst the names of painters that must certainly be listed as having drawn inspiration from them are William Allan (1782–1850), John Clerk of Eldin (1728–1812), Joseph Farington (1747–1821), James Giles (1801–70), Horatio McCulloch (1805–67), Jacob Moore (1740–93), Alexander Nasmyth (1758–1840), John Runciman (1744–68), John Thomas (1813–62) and Joseph Mallord William Turner (1775–1851). In most of their paintings it was perhaps more the picturesque than the sublime qualities that were represented, as seen in Thomson's almost obsessive series of studies of Fast Castle (East Lothian). In Nasmyth's study of Tantallon (East Lothian), however, it is the sublime qualities of the ruin-capped beetling cliffs around which stormy seas are breaking that are most evident (Fig 2.17).

The Gothic Revival and the retention of earlier buildings

A combination of respect for the castles of one's real or adopted ancestors, together with a rapidly increasing admiration for the types of historic architecture that could be recognised by one's peers as either picturesque or sublime, was a heady mixture. In their time Robert Adam's castles had perhaps been a relatively exceptional response to the slightly rarefied tastes of an enlightened few, though by the early decades of the 19th century medieval architectural styles were becoming very much more generally favoured as the Gothic Revival gathered momentum. In addition to growing numbers of new houses designed in what was meant to be a medieval idiom, many houses continued to be extended around the preserved nucleus of a medieval tower and its associated buildings, and the process of retention inevitably entailed a greater or lesser measure of repair to the historic fabric.

At Dundas Castle (West Lothian) there is an imposing L-plan tower for which a licence had been granted in 1424, and which had been augmented or remodelled

Figure 2.18 Airth
Castle, the junction
of the old and new
buildings

on a number of occasions. The tower itself had been enlarged by the addition of a
new wing, and early views show that there was an extensive courtyard contained
within crenellated and towered walls, inside which a large-scale residential range
of possibly early 17th-century date had been built. In the early 19th century
James Dundas decided to provide himself and his new wife with a more spacious
modern residence than they could in fact afford, but there seems never to have
been any question of demolishing the old tower in doing so. His architect was
William Burn, whose earliest proposals involved the retention of much of the old
complex, with the tower at the very heart of the expanded building, behind a new
entrance front. This was a similar approach to that which Burn was taking in his
designs of 1817 for the Fletcher family at Saltoun (East Lothian). By 1818, however,
it had been decided that only the tower should be retained at Dundas, and that
it was to be associated with a service courtyard to one side of a completely new
house in a Gothic style. Perhaps to justify its retention, the tower was fitted out
as a distillery, though this mundane use certainly did not mean that it was not
an important element in the new architectural composition; in fact it probably
figured more prominently in this modified arrangement than would have been
the case if it had been absorbed – and largely hidden – within the body of the
new house.

There were almost as many ways for the retention of an earlier castle to be
accomplished as there were cases of doing so. At the Graham family's Airth
Castle (Stirlingshire), for example, in 1807 David Hamilton left the right-angled
arrangement of tower and later ranges largely untouched in the greatly enlarged
house (Fig 2.18). The result, which was perhaps in some ways related to what
had been proposed for Barnbougle, was a triangular plan that had a handsomely

symmetrical new towered and crenellated range across the third side of the triangle, but with a graceful top-lit semi-circular saloon at the heart. It may be significant that in the distant views of the house across the plains of the Forth valley it is the earlier buildings that are most in evidence. At Hoddom Castle (Dumfriesshire), a massive mid-16th-century L-plan tower built for Sir John Maxwell, with its wing heightened around the 1630s, was retained as the very evident centrepiece of a series of 19th-century enlargements that resulted in a house of enormous scale (see Fig 3.11). The first of these, which involved the demolition of a number of buildings other than the tower, was carried out for General Matthew Sharpe to the designs of William Burn in 1826 and there were further major additions for Edward Brook in 1878. But in all of this there was no doubt that the 16th-century tower was the fulcrum and governing feature, even though the rooms it contained were no longer of high status in the new domestic arrangements.

Elsewhere, the earlier work might be permitted a less obvious, though nevertheless seminal, presence. At Loudon Castle (Ayrshire), which was rebuilt in 1804–11 by Archibald Elliot for the future Marquess of Hastings, the earlier work was retained within an enormous new quadrangular house that is said to have cost an eye-watering £100,000 before work had to be stopped (Fig 2.19). The tower that was the earliest part of the ancestral home of the marchioness's family was retained in the east range, at the rear of the house, while a later part formed the basis for the adjacent south range. Externally, the earlier work was so extensively refaced and remodelled that there was little evidence of it, though the presence of the tower was proclaimed by a three-storeyed superstructure that was raised on top of it.

At Dunrobin (Sutherland), the historic seat of the Earls, and later the Dukes of Sutherland, a dynasty that traced its ancestry back to the 12th century, even more of the earlier castle was retained than at Loudon in the course of a

Figure 2.19 Loudon Castle (© RCAHMS. DP 023965, Licensor www.rcahms.gov.uk)

Figure 2.20 Dunrobin
Castle, the earlier
work is to the left
in this aerial view
(© RCAHMS. SC
873693, Licensor
www.rcahms.gov.uk)

grandiloquent enlargement carried out to the designs of Charles Barry between 1844 and 1850 (Fig 2.20). The earliest part of the building as it existed before that operation is assumed to be a small rectangular tower that is probably of the 15th century, though earlier dates have been suggested for it. In the 1640s two L-shaped residential ranges were added on different axes from the tower, which were connected to the tower by a circular stair turret. Between 1720 and 1740 plans for further additions were made, and a south range with thinner walls may be of that period; there were more additions in about 1785 and 1835. The scale of this complex was, however, completely dwarfed by Barry's extensions, in which the almost unparalleled wealth of the Sutherland family meant that no expense was spared, at a time when they were also building on a grand scale at Trentham, Cliveden, and at Lancaster House in the heart of London. Under the circumstances, it might have been expected that, as at Loudon, the earlier work would have been completely remodelled so that it was in greater architectural accord with the additions. However, although the topography of the promontory site meant that the early tower had to be enclosed within a new courtyard, the ranges associated with it remained clearly expressed on the south and west sides of the castle in its final polygonal form. It was also intended that the rooms within those ranges should be fitted out for exalted use, with the duke's apartment in the south range, and his heir's in the west range. There could be little doubt that the visible retention of the ancestral seat, and the clear expression of that retention, were important factors in the design of the new work.

By the mid-19th century, the gathering momentum of interest in medieval architecture, and of its applicability to the design of great houses in Scotland, had been given greatly enhanced acceptability in a number of ways. Between 1817 and 1823 Sir Walter Scott, who had probably done more than any other individual to foster popular interest in the Middle Ages, and whose poetry has already been quoted, remodelled his home at Abbotsford to the designs of William Atkinson. In doing so he drew much of his inspiration from the nearby abbey of Melrose, and, though the results were thus perhaps more monastic than castellated in character, the example he set did much to encourage others to adopt medieval architectural forms. Some decades afterwards, a more authoritative basis for the understanding and emulation of the Scottish architectural vocabulary was provided by the four volumes of exquisite engravings of potential exemplars in Robert William Billings's *Baronial and ecclesiastical antiquities of Scotland*, which were published between 1845 and 1852. The examples provided in those volumes made it possible for architects such as William Burn and James Gillespie Graham to design and restore castles in a more 'correctly Scottish' idiom, as opposed to the vaguely 'Tudorbethan' forms that had previously tended to prevail. Subsequently, between 1853 and 1855, a royal seal of approval was given to the re-creation of such architecture when Queen Victoria and Prince Albert had their Highland home at Balmoral rebuilt on a fresh site and on a vast scale to the baronialising designs of William Smith. If it was thus made even more acceptable to live in a house that had the external appearance of a castle, the case for retaining an existing real castle when a residence was to be remodelled had become almost unassailable.

CHAPTER 3

The emergence of new attitudes

The restoration of castles to a historic state

In many of the cases considered in the later parts of the previous chapter, the historic structures of the castles became just one element within a far greater whole, not unlike the grain of sand around which a pearl develops. As a result of such operations, the early buildings might be almost completely lost to sight, as at Culzean and Loudon (see Figs 2.9–2.10 and 2.19), or they might be allowed varying degrees of continued expression, as at Hoddom and Dunrobin (see Figs 3.11 and 2.20). It must be conceded that the great scale of the additions frequently meant that the historic structures became a subordinate component, but the retained structures were presumably seen as giving the authority of antiquity to the expanded complex. Approaches of these kinds continued to be followed at many subsequent projects. In parallel with those approaches, however, the progressive emergence of a more scholarly and analytical understanding of medieval architecture meant that a growing number of castle owners – or potential owners – wished to live in buildings that reflected their historic state more authentically, or at least more sympathetically.

At the same time, growing numbers of owners were beginning to take a more active approach towards the preservation of castles on their estates, even when there was no intention of their being brought back into any sort of use. Many castles had suffered from the pilfering of their more recyclable building materials, and especially the dressed stone used for quoins, doorways, windows, fireplaces and stairways, while most castles that were no longer inhabited had lost the timberwork of floors and roofs either through decay or theft. Such robbing of materials had left large numbers of castles in a precarious state. In the course of the 19th century, however, limited 'lairdish' repairs were increasingly instigated on a growing number of estates. At many sites there is still clear evidence of how walls above fireplaces have been supported by inserted relieving arches where lintels had been removed, or how the flanks of doorways and windows have been strengthened by rubble insertions to replace the robbed-out jambs. At Old Castle Lachlan (Argyll), for example, it can even be seen how, in an attempt to forestall further collapse, stairwells, doorways and windows have been simply blocked up. Linked in with works of this kind was often the aim of making the ruins more accessible and safer for visitors, and especially for those from a nearby great house where the owners of the ruins themselves often now lived. At Loch Leven (Kinross-shire) (see Fig 2.12), where we have already seen that the late

17th-century Kinross House had been aligned on the ruins of the island castle, new access to the tower was provided in the form of a basement entrance and a permanent stair to the floor above, while parapets were built around the walk along the top of the curtain wall.

Buildings as authentic representatives of the past

By the middle years of the 19th century the idea that some old buildings might be so individually significant that they should not be subjected to works that would detract from their essential character was coming to have a wider currency. This idea was not new; it is one that can be traced back to antiquity, though it appears to have assumed an enhanced and more fully documented importance in the Renaissance. In 1462, for example, as his concern for the loss of the remains of ancient Rome increased, Pope Pius II had ordered:

> … we desire that the antique and early buildings remain for future generations … we formally forbid all … to dare to demolish, destroy, reduce, break down … any ancient public building or the remains of any public building …

As has been outlined in the previous chapter, however, the attitudes which more specifically underlie those of our own generation began to assume greater definition from the 18th century onwards. So far as castles are concerned, in parallel with the fascination for their picturesque qualities, the growth of scholarly interest in the history and material remains of the Middle Ages that was then emerging led to a greater respect for what had survived. This in turn fostered an awareness of the need to bring back into a state of repair buildings that were themselves a very important form of primary evidence for the Middle Ages, but that might have been neglected for centuries.

The architects who were first entrusted with work of this kind were generally uninhibited by any sense of the need to conserve everything that they found, or by any view that minimal disturbance of the surviving historic state should be a leading aspiration. Few of these architects appear to have felt a need for false modesty, and most seem to have considered that their own contribution was fully as valid as that of their predecessors; indeed, many perhaps considered that their work might even represent an improvement on what already existed. There was initially only limited appreciation of the fact that, whatever their perceived aesthetic merits or demerits, these buildings were documents that embodied fragile and altogether irreplaceable evidence for our understanding of architecture at the periods which produced them.

Such cavalier attitudes on the part of some architects led in due course to a backlash as those contributing to the developing strand of antiquarian interest in the buildings viewed with dismay some of the more invasive restorations that were being carried out. At a time when private property rights were regarded as absolutely inviolable, and much of what took place behind estate walls remained largely unseen, this backlash emerged initially as a response to the more visible campaigns that were being carried out at the great cathedrals of England. At several of those, long periods of poor maintenance were beginning to call forth an energetic response that in some cases was excessively draconian. In an address to the Society of Antiquaries of London in 1795 about James Wyatt's work on Durham Cathedral, for example, John Carter said:

> To regret the devastation continually making in our cathedrals … will itself be of no avail, unless some efforts of laudable and animated zeal be made for the preservation of the remaining ones … The … patron of this society should be implored to stay in time this innovating rage and prevent interested persons from effacing the still remembered unaltered traits of our ancient magnificence which are but faintly imitated and perhaps never to be equalled.

In Scotland, a parallel stance is to be seen some decades later in the advice of Robert Reid, the king's Master of Works. North of the Border, because of what happened in the aftermath of the Reformation, the Crown had rather loosely defined rights in many monasteries and at a number of the churches that had served as cathedrals and, in reporting on the work to be carried out on Dunfermline Abbey by the state in 1829, Reid argued:

> I conceive that in all cases of this kind restoration or embellishment should not be the object, but that repairs … should be executed … with the view solely to their preservation, and in effecting that object the less appearance of interference with their present state and construction the better.

The call for a more conservative approach, in which preservation of the buildings as authentic representatives of the past was seen as paramount, was clearly gathering greater momentum by the mid-19th century. Indeed, by 1855 the executive committee on restoration of the Society of Antiquaries of London considered it had to make a stand by saying that, if things continued as they were: 'the monumental remains … will, before long, cease to exist as truthful records of the past'.

Perhaps the most passionately articulated expression of this view was that offered by William Morris, who, in his manifesto at the time of the foundation of the Society for the Protection of Ancient Buildings in 1877, urged that we should: 'treat our ancient buildings as monuments of bygone art, created by bygone manners, that modern art cannot meddle with without destroying'.

Ten years after Morris published his manifesto, the understanding of castles in Scotland began to be entirely transformed through the publication of the first of a series of five volumes with the title *The castellated and domestic architecture of Scotland*, the last of which appeared in 1892. This extraordinary scholarly achievement, which provided an illustrated account of the vast majority of buildings that might be described as castles, was the work of two indefatigable authors, David MacGibbon and Thomas Ross. The books immediately became an essential point of reference, providing authoritative information on the full range of secular architecture between the 12th and 17th centuries. It might be added that, although recent research has further developed our understanding in many directions, the five volumes remain the standard survey of Scottish castles.

The restoration of castles for renewed use

The shift in attitudes and understanding that was taking place in the later 19th century was to have a considerable impact on the way castles were treated. While a major driving force continued to be the wish to restore or expand an ancestral home, there might also be other motives for undertaking work. On an exposed hill-top site on the Minto estate in the Scottish Borders there is a small 16th-century rectangular tower that was built for the Turnbull family, which rejoices in the name of Fatlips Castle (Roxburghshire) (Fig 3.1). Such a diminutive building could never have been considered as even an occasional residence for the later owners of the estate, the Earls of Minto, but its prominent location on Minto Craigs made it an obvious eye-catcher within the landscape of the estate, and it could also be used as a shooting box. It was as such that it was restored in 1857 to the designs of the architect William Anderson, at which time it was given a rather more enriched superstructure than such an unambitious tower was ever likely to have had, in order to give an enhanced interest to the skyline. A parapet with angle rounds, carried on three-stage corbels, and with water spouts in the form of cannon, projects boldly outwards, behind which there is a garret storey lit by dormer windows, within crow-stepped gables. The silhouette is further enriched by a circular cap house to the spiral stair and a pair of chimney stacks to the gables. In the course of a second phase of works, in 1897, the interior was fitted out with ribbed ceilings and wainscot panelling, and it was decided that the tower should also serve as a small

Figure 3.1 Fatlips Castle

Figure 3.2 Duart
Castle (© RCAHMS.
SC 581222, Licensor
www.rcahms.gov.uk)

estate museum; this later work was carried out by Robert Lorimer, who was undertaking various works at Minto House itself at the time.

Family connections with a particular site were often one of the strongest reasons for carrying out the restoration of a long-abandoned castle, and this has perhaps tended to be more true in the Highland areas than the Lowlands, where clan loyalties – or perhaps sometimes a slightly romanticised vision of such loyalties – might continue to carry great weight. One of the most dramatic restorations was carried out at Duart (Argyll), which is sited on a rock promontory at the westernmost point of the island of Mull, where it appears to grow almost organically out of the rock (Fig 3.2). It is thought to have been first built for the MacDougall lords of Lorne, but its constableship, and subsequently its ownership, were acquired by the MacLean family in 1390. Despite the fact that by 1674 the castle and estates had passed into the acquisitive hands of the ninth Earl of Argyll, it continued to be viewed as their historic base by later generations of MacLeans.

The starting point for the medieval and early modern architectural development of the site was a roughly rectangular enclosure defined by massively constructed curtain walls, within which there would presumably have been less substantially built ranges around at least some of the sides. That first castle was presumably built by the MacDougalls in the 13th century, and in its original form it shows a related approach to the choice of site and architectural design as the MacDougall castle of Dunstaffnage, albeit without the latter's corner towers. A rectangular tower house of even more massive construction than the courtyard walls was added against its north-west side around the late 14th century, presumably after the castle and lands had passed to the MacLeans. Entrance to that tower was at ground-floor level, through its north-east face, where the doorway was protected by a single-storey forebuilding that had a postern door at its outer end. There was evidently a separate entrance to the first floor of the tower, and a stair from there to the upper floors. At subsequent dates the north-east curtain wall was rebuilt, as were the ranges along the south-east and north-east sides of the courtyard. The former range appears to be largely of the 16th century, while the latter bears the date 1673 and the initials of Sir Allan MacLean, which is perhaps a little surprising, since the Earl of Argyll was already beginning to take steps to wrest the estate from him by that date.

Despite being no longer in his family's ownership, Duart castle was garrisoned by Sir John MacLean in 1692, as part of his opposition to the Revolution settlement that brought King William and Queen Mary to the throne, and he was subsequently forced to flee into exile in France. A Board of Ordnance survey of 1741 shows the castle in a slightly unkempt state. Nevertheless, it was to be occupied by government troops during the Jacobite Rising of 1745–46, though this may not have been a comfortable experience for them, since by 1748 it was said that the roofs were ruinous, and that repairs costed at £1500 were required. In that same year a survey by Paul Sandby depicted the castle in the early stages of its ruination, albeit in an altogether more picturesque light than had the coolly dispassionate survey of 1741.

In view of its state by the mid-18th century, it is perhaps not surprising that nothing was done to bring the castle back into repair for one and a half centuries. The tide only turned in 1911, when it was bought back by the MacLean family, in the person of Sir Fitzroy MacLean, the long-lived 26th Chief of the Clan, and tenth baronet, who had the remarkable distinction of having been a hussar with the Light Brigade in the Crimea. MacLean engaged the architect J J Burnet of Glasgow to carry out a full restoration, which was based at least in part on a report on the building prepared by Thomas Ross and Alfred Lightly MacGibbon. This work was completed in almost record time by the following year. It is difficult to avoid the conclusion that a castle built on an exposed rock outcrop, high above the meeting point of frequently stormy waters, and contained within the limits of massively constructed curtain walls, could not lend itself readily to the ideas of domestic comfort and convenience held by most people living in the 20th century. But there can be no doubt that both MacLean and Burnet were overwhelmingly anxious to preserve the 'castle air' of Duart so far as was possible, and that is what is so wonderfully evocative about their achievement in the views of it as seen on the approach to Mull by sea from Oban.

When faced with the conflicting demands of preserving architectural evidence on the one hand and of making the castle sufficiently habitable for a modern family on the other, however, it is almost inevitable that on some points it is the latter that must take precedence in a building with such a defined character. The glazed platform that was created at first-floor level off the north-east end of the tower house, for example, while providing astonishing views from within the castle, might be seen as detracting from the sense of enclosure that is such a dominant characteristic of a castle of this kind, whilst within the courtyard the projecting bay that was formed at the southern end of the tower house perhaps has a slightly over-domestic appearance in such a context. Within the tower house, the way in which the floor level of the first-floor hall has been modified to create more acceptable proportions for modern tastes creates some inconsistencies in the relationship of the window embrasures to the new floor. Nevertheless, in planning the restoration of Duart, Burnet had been faced with an extremely difficult task, and it says much for his skills that the results are as successful as they indeed are.

At precisely the same time that J J Burnet was restoring the wind-beaten walls of Duart, the architect Robert Lorimer, who had earlier worked at Fatlips (see Fig 3.1), was called in to restore another Argyll castle. That castle was Dunderave, a sophisticated L-plan house built in 1598 for John MacNaughton on the rather mellower shores of Loch Fyne, which had survived virtually complete to the wall head (Fig 3.3). With its spacious spiral stair in an extrusion within the re-entrant angle running the full height of the building's five storeys, and a large round tower at the diagonally opposite corner, its layout was of a type that could lend itself to comfortable modern occupation with minimal modifications. In 1911 Miss Noble, a member of the family that had built a new house at Ardkinglas on the opposite shore of Loch Fyne in 1906–08, decided to restore it for her own use. It was hardly surprising that she called upon the architect who had designed such a wonderful house at Ardkinglas to work for her at Dunderave.

The adaptability to modern needs of the planning of the existing late 16th-century house, together with its structural completeness, meant that Lorimer was able to adopt a rather less creative approach than was sometimes his wont in dealing with historic buildings. The principal physical changes were those that were required to establish connections with the additional ranges that Miss Noble's way of life required, and that were considered necessary to

Figure 3.3 Dunderave Castle (© RCAHMS. SC 559841, Licensor www.rcahms.gov.uk)

re-create the courtyard of buildings that would always have accompanied such a house. In designing these new ranges, Lorimer displayed a keen sensitivity both to the irregular contours of the site, and to the need to make the new work clearly subservient to the original building. The solution adopted was to have two new pairs of ranges. An entrance range, on the south side of the courtyard, was connected to the wing of the original house by a narrower range that was opened up at first-floor level as a delightful westward-facing loggia looking down the loch. On this side the new work was set at a slight angle to the tower. To the east of the tower a lower L-shaped pair of one-and-a-half-storey ranges was built to contain the service accommodation. In all of this, as might be expected from an architect who was such a keen supporter of the re-establishment of craft skills, Lorimer took the greatest care to match the materials and character of the masonry throughout. While purists might regret the decision not to reinstate the external render, and might even regard it as an aspect of what has sometimes been dismissed as 'rubblemania', it could certainly be argued that the exposed stonework helped to establish a more intimate relationship with a landscape setting in which rock outcrops figure so prominently.

In 1911, neither Lorimer nor his client saw any inconsistency in making quite substantial – albeit subservient – additions to Dunderave to ensure that it could meet the domestic requirements of the time. But such attitudes were already being questioned by some. Indeed, in commissioning John Currie to restore Kellie Castle (Fife) in 1878, Lorimer's own father had gone to considerable lengths to ensure that it was the building itself that governed the way of life within it, rather than the family's way of life that was taken as justification for changes to the building. The shift of attitudes is perhaps most clearly epitomised in the Hon. Clive Pearson's rejection of Lorimer's proposals from the 1920s for the restoration of Castle Fraser (Aberdeenshire), on the grounds that his family should fit within the castle as it stood rather than expect the castle to be adapted to their needs (see Fig 24.1).

One of the most thorough-going attempts to recreate the medieval form of a castle was carried out for Lord Howard de Walden at Dean (Ayrshire), on the outskirts of Kilmarnock, which had been in the continuous possession of the Boyd family from 1316 until it was partly gutted by fire in 1735 (see Fig 1.11). The earliest part of the complex is a rectangular tower house, which could be as old as the later part of the 14th century on the basis of the battered plinth, limited fenestration and simple treatment of the wall head. In the 15th century, perhaps not long after the time that Robert Boyd was summoned as a Lord of parliament in 1459, a spacious range was added, with what appears to have been a sequence of hall and outer and inner chambers on the principal floor, above a kitchen and other offices at ground-floor level; a tower with a machicolated parapet was provided above the inner chamber. In the time of the Lord Boyd who died in 1654, this range was augmented on the courtyard side by the addition of a forebuilding and the provision of new fenestration. After passing through various hands following the fire of 1735, the castle was acquired in 1828 by Lord Howard de Walden, and in 1905 the eighth holder of that title determined to restore the castle, in a leisurely process that was to last for over 30 years.

The first part to be restored was the tower house, where the work was under the supervision of Henry Brown of Kilmarnock. When work moved on to the hall and chamber range, the shell of which was largely complete, the greatest care was taken in establishing the most appropriate form for the wall-head detailing; photographs taken in 1914 appear to show that a length of parapet, together with attic gablets, had been mocked up in timber and canvas to ensure that the proportions were acceptable. The architect of this stage of works is not known with certainty, but James S Richardson, who was appointed as the first, part-time, Inspector of Ancient Monuments for Scotland in 1914 (and who was thus the lineal ancestor of the current Historic Scotland Inspectorate), was certainly in charge of one phase, at a time when he was also a partner in the firm of Richardson and McKay. The approach taken in the hall and chamber range would be consistent with his drive for a high measure of archaeological accuracy. On the basis of dates on the internal plasterwork, the fitting out of the range was being completed in the 1930s, progress having been interrupted by the Great War. One of the final, and perhaps slightly unexpected, touches was the addition of a gatehouse inspired by that of the nearby castle of Rowallan, which bears the date 1936–37. The end result at Dean is a careful recreation of the main buildings, with just enough of a sense of chivalric romanticism to raise it above the pedestrian and give an element of zest. How far the restored castle was ever intended to function as a modern residence for its owner is unclear, however, since he appears to have continued to occupy a range of 18th- and 19th-century date on the opposite side of the courtyard from the hall and chamber. The restored parts of the castle were probably chiefly intended to provide a suitable home for Lord Howard's fine collection of musical instruments and armour, as well as a location for occasional social functions.

In the examples considered so far in this chapter, there was sufficient surviving historic fabric to act as the governing factor in the process of restoration, and, where additions were made, there was generally a painstaking effort to ensure that they were subordinate to the historic fabric and that they respected its idiom. In a number of cases, however, a site was chosen – sometimes for the beauty of its setting as much as for the interest of its architecture – where the structural remains were so fragmentary that there could be little question of authentic restoration. In such cases a building that is essentially a new creation must inevitably be the result. Perhaps the supreme example of that approach is Eilean Donan Castle (Ross-shire) (Figs 3.4 and 3.5).

The castle at Eilean Donan, which stands on a tidal island off the shore of Loch Duich where there had once been a prehistoric fort, may have been established from as early as the 13th century; there was certainly a castle in existence at the time of a visit by the Earl of Moray in 1331, when it was in the possession of the MacKenzie family. A Board of Ordnance drawing of 1714 by Lewis Petit shows that in its final form the main enclosure was of irregular polygonal plan, with walls following the outline of the higher part of the island. There was a substantially constructed tower on the north side, and a more lightly built L-shaped residential block at the south-west corner. There was also a smaller rectangular building

Figure 3.4 Eilean
Donan Castle
before restoration
(© RCAHMS. SC
498060, Licensor
www.rcahms.gov.uk)

Figure 3.5 Eilean
Donan Castle (Dara
Parsons)

on the opposite side of the courtyard from the main tower, and an irregular
hexagonal enclosure at the east end, which has been described as a water cistern
but which was probably designed as a defensive feature associated with the main
entrance to the courtyard. There is evidence that the enclosure had at one stage
been rather more extensive, with rectangular towers at some of the changes of
angle. Shortly after Petit's drawing had been made, when the castle was occupied
by Spanish troops who had arrived in support of an ill-conceived Jacobite rising in
1719, the castle was subjected to a bombardment by two government frigates, and

the Spaniards' powder magazine was blown up, leaving the castle in an extremely fragmentary state.

Having languished in a state of advanced ruination for almost two centuries, the castle was acquired and rebuilt between 1912 and 1932 to the designs of George Mackie Watson, for Lieutenant-Colonel John MacRae-Gilstrap. By that stage there was insufficient physical evidence for accurate reconstruction, and there was as yet no knowledge of the 1714 Board of Ordnance record drawing. The basis of the reconstruction is said to have been a vivid dream by one Farquhar MacRae. The result is a lyrical idyll of extraordinary charm on the theme of an architectural past that can never have been, within a landscape setting that could hardly be surpassed for its beauty. In a sense it is a smaller-scale Scottish equivalent of the dream castle that King Ludwig II of Bavaria created at Neuschwanstein between 1869 and 1886. In neither case are the results more than a partial reflection of buildings that once existed; yet, although the adopted approach to rebuilding is not one that would now be advocated for buildings of great historic or architectural significance, the world would certainly be a poorer place without at least a few such castles.

The preservation of castles as 'monuments'

However, as has already been said, by the later 19th century an awareness of the potential for historic buildings to provide primary evidence for the ages that produced them was gaining wider acceptance: it is thus hardly surprising that in some cases a castle might be restored or conserved because of its perceived significance in the history of the nation. Perhaps the best known case of this is some of the work that was carried out at Edinburgh Castle in the later 19th century. Since the early 17th century, when the castle had lost its royal function following the departure of Scotland's kings for London, it had come to be valued chiefly for its strategically important role as a military barrack. Many of the historic buildings within it were consequently adapted to meet that need, while new buildings, although generally handsomely enough proportioned and detailed, were as a matter of necessity designed to serve their military function as efficiently as possible. The early 12th-century chapel had been adapted as a magazine and lost to sight, while from 1650 the great hall had been transformed to serve as a barrack, with additional floors and cross walls inserted in 1737. In the course of the later 19th century, however, there was a growing sense that greater respect should be accorded to the castle which figured so prominently in a physical sense on Edinburgh's skyline, and so warmly in a spiritual sense in Scotland's view of itself as a nation.

From the early 19th century the castle was thus increasingly coming to be seen as a national monument. The rediscovered Scottish regalia had been on display in the castle since 1818; in 1829 the great 15th-century bombard Mons Meg, which had been a gift of the Duke of Burgundy to James II, had been returned from the Tower of London; and in 1845 the chapel was identified as such, with a first restoration being carried out in 1851 (Fig 3.6). By 1877 it was decided it would be best if the chapel and the parts of the palace that had become popularly associated with Mary Queen of Scots should be transferred from the War Office to the care of the Office of Works (the ancestor of the Ministry of Works and ultimately of Historic Scotland). But there were also at least some within the military establishment who wished to see a more historically sensitive approach taken to such a nationally significant complex of buildings, chief amongst whom was Major Gore Booth of the Royal Engineers.

By 1885 Gore Booth had persuaded William Nelson, a wealthy publisher, to sponsor the restoration of the great hall, the chapel and the portcullis gate, to the designs of the architect Hippolyte Blanc. The discussion associated with all this work offers a fascinating glimpse into the increasingly conservation-minded attitudes relating to the preservation of historic buildings that were emerging around this time. This is perhaps best seen in the way that Daniel Wilson, who had earlier identified the chapel, argued:

> The work of restoration of an ancient historical building … ought to be carried out in the most conservative spirit. What is wanted is not a fine building, with all possible modern additions; but the original, or a facsimile of it in any effaced portions.

Figure 3.6 Edinburgh Castle chapel (© Crown copyright)

Eventually it was decided that no further work should be carried out on the chapel; for the portcullis gate and great hall, however, an altogether more creative path was to be followed than that advocated by Wilson. So far as the gate was concerned, much of the superstructure added in 1584 to the gate of 1577 had been destroyed in the 18th century, and the slightly arbitrary decision was taken to give the upper parts something of the appearance of a tower house. To guide the work on the great hall, which had been built for James IV in the years to either side of 1500, there was a detailed Board of Ordnance survey that showed its state in 1754 (Fig 3.7). Blanc, however, appears to have regarded those drawings and the surviving structure itself as little more than factors to be taken into account in drawing up his designs. Consequently, as completed by him in 1891, the interior was essentially an impressive late Victorian space, with a magnificent fireplace copied from one at Crichton Castle,

Figure 3.7 Edinburgh Castle, a survey of the hall based on the 1754 Board of Ordnance survey (© RCAHMS. DP 078949, Licensor www.rcahms.gov.uk)

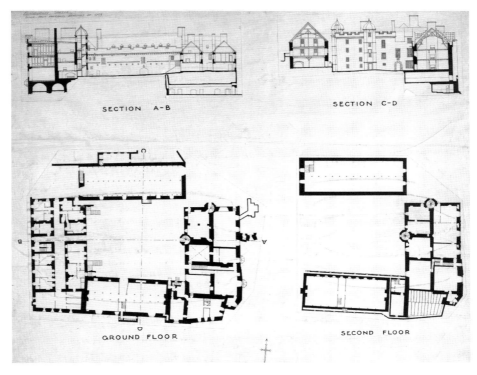

SECTION A-B

SECTION C-D

GROUND FLOOR

SECOND FLOOR

Figure 3.8 Edinburgh Castle, the hall as restored (© Crown copyright)

and with great expanses of wainscotting and much heraldic stained glass. Virtually the only broadly original feature is the heavily restored hammer-beam roof. Judged as such, the restored hall is a fine achievement. Assessed as a medieval royal great hall, however, it is difficult not to feel a sense of disappointment at what has been so evidently lost, as well as at the slightly sterile appearance of the new masonry and woodwork (Fig 3.8).

Conservation as a monument, with a prime aim of ensuring that the surviving historic fabric of a building would be passed on to future generations with minimal loss of evidence, had been Daniel Wilson's aspiration for Edinburgh's chapel. It was also increasingly an approach adopted by private individuals. As early as about 1830, for example, the eighth Earl of Wemyss had repaired and reroofed his castle at Elcho (Perthshire), where he had a particular interest since the barony of that place was the courtesy title of his heir. In some cases an enlightened owner might decide to open his castle to the public after stabilising the ruins of its historic fabric. At Edzell, for example (see Figs 1.10 and 2.1), after this had been done in 1853 by Lord Panmure, the future eleventh Earl of Dalhousie, we are told that 'countless numbers of tourists hailing from all parts of the globe … visited the historic pile'. By 1897 an enterprising local author had decided to produce an excellent and fully indexed guidebook to the castle, with 90 pages of text that might provide a useful model for many modern guidebook writers who set their sights on a less demanding level of readership.

A particularly active conserver and restorer of ancient buildings was the third Marquess of Bute. Rothesay Castle (Bute), which had been held by his ancestors (who were also amongst the ancestors of the royal family of Scotland) since the time when the island was seized from the kings of Norway in the 13th century, was of particular importance for the Bute Stewarts. It had been first built with an unusual circular curtain wall not long after the island had been taken from the king of Norway, and it was probably after an abortive attempt to retake the castle by the Norwegians in 1266 that four semi-circular towers were added around its periphery. Initially, the residential buildings appear to have been almost randomly spread around the circular courtyard, but at the turn of the 15th and 16th centuries an imposing forebuilding was added on the north side of the curtain wall, which had the principal entrance to the castle at its lowest level and handsome lodgings fit for royal occupation above (Fig 3.9).

The castle had been burnt and rendered uninhabitable by the Duke of Argyll in 1685, but as early as 1816 the second Marquess of Bute gave orders for the courtyard to be tidied up by the removal of collapsed rubble and vegetation. Perhaps unsurprisingly, however, it was the fabulously wealthy third Marquess, who had an almost fanatical interest in the Middle Ages, who initiated a major operation of consolidation and partial restoration of the building. In the 1870s he commissioned William Burges to carry out an analytical study of Rothesay and to start the process of consolidating the fabric. Burges was the architect of the enchanting recreations of Cardiff Castle in 1868–85 and Castell Coch in 1875–79, Bute's principal Welsh properties. By comparison with what was done at those castles, the work at Rothesay was a very conservative operation, aimed essentially at stabilising the remains and preventing further decay. In 1900, however, Bute decided to reconstruct in part the forebuilding that had been built by James IV and James V. The rebuilt fabric, which was executed under the supervision of J R Thomson, was carefully distinguished from the historic structure by the use of red sandstone, a demonstration of Lord Bute's anxiety to ensure that there should be no confusion of the historic evidence for those who were sufficiently interested to wish to understand the castle.

From 1887 the Marquess of Bute was also Keeper of the royal palace of Falkland, where most of what is now seen had been built in two phases for James IV and James V between 1501 and 1542. There had already been some restoration for a previous owner in 1824, with more in the years around 1840. After 1887, however, Lord Bute brought his customary energy (and great wealth) to dealing with the palace, in the course of which there was a generally sensitive restoration of the habitable south quarter, under the direction of the architect

John Kinross. There was also extensive reconstruction of missing masonry in the
east range, where the royal lodgings had been located, and which had been burnt
out in 1654 by Cromwellian troops. Bute's activity at Falkland was not limited to
the upstanding parts of the building, however. He also excavated the foundations
of the great hall, which formed the north quarter of the palace's main close,
and traced the partial foundations of the 13th-century castle of the Earls of Fife
further to the north. Once these features had been exposed, rather than restore
them, he treated them as parts of what by that time would be referred to as a
'monument', outlining the plan of the hall with dwarf walls, and consolidating the
exposed footings of the two towers of the castle that had been exposed.

At Cardiff Castle and Castell Coch, Bute had been the prime mover behind two of the most wonderful Gothic architectural fantasies to be raised in late 19th-century Europe; he was also the patron of one of the most opulent essays in medievalising domestic architecture in the house he rebuilt on his ancestral estate at Mount Stuart on Bute. And yet in parts of Rothesay Castle and Falkland Palace (and as can also be seen in his partial reconstruction of the east and south claustral ranges of St Andrews Cathedral Priory) he demonstrated another side to his love of medieval architecture, in the immense care he took not to detract from the story that buildings he regarded as 'monuments' could tell about their first state. In these latter cases, the way in which he used a different stone for all new masonry that his architects deemed it necessary to insert shows a keen awareness of ideas on architectural conservation that were gaining greater acceptance at that time. The advocates of those ideas urged that, at monuments of great significance, on close inspection there should be no scope for confusion between what was essentially primary structural evidence and what was prosthetic insertion.

As we have seen, the third Marquess of Bute was by no means alone in taking active steps to conserve historic castles in his ownership as monuments of the ages that had produced them. Amongst a number of other examples of such interventions was the work of the Earl of Moray at Doune Castle (Perthshire), which had a particular significance for that family since the heir to the earldom bore the courtesy title of Lord Doune. This magnificent courtyard castle, which may have originated in the late 13th century but which had been largely rebuilt a century later for the Duke of Albany, had passed to the ancestors of the Earls of Moray in the late 16th century. Although the castle had ceased to be a primary residence for the family as early as the 17th century, it was kept in a good state for many years afterwards, with costly repairs to the roofs being undertaken in 1729. Despite that, however, the castle had become a roofless shell by the end of the 18th century, and it was the fourteenth earl who in 1883 engaged the Office of Works architect Andrew Kerr to reinstate the roofs and carry out necessary repairs (Fig 3.10). As part of this operation a number of works were carried out that were perhaps closer to what we would now think of as restoration rather than simple conservation, including the insertion of a screen and tiled floors in what had probably been the Duke of Albany's

Figure 3.10 Doune Castle (© Crown copyright)

chamber. Nevertheless, there was no intention of restoring the castle to a habitable state, and the guiding aim was essentially to preserve the fabric for future generations, to make it safe for those who wished to visit it, and to offer some hints as to how it would have been fitted out.

The recent legislative background to work on castles and the provision of grant assistance

In 1984 Doune Castle was placed in the care of the state, and at this point it is perhaps appropriate to say something about the historic and current role of the government in the care of castles. As early as the first Ancient Monuments Act of 1882 it had been envisaged that the state might take ancient sites and structures into its care, though it was expected that in most cases their legal ownership would remain unchanged. At that stage it was mainly archaeological monuments that were seen as candidates for such protection, though in 1900 this possibility was extended to later monuments, and as a result state care has so far been provided for about 70 of Scotland's most significant castles, the majority of which are opened to the public on a regular basis.

But the state also began to extend its interest to buildings where the onus of maintenance continued to rest with the owners. In 1913 the Ancient Monuments Consolidation and Amendment Act required the Commissioners of Works to prepare lists of 'such monuments as are reported by the Ancient Monuments Board as being monuments the preservation of which is of national importance'. This was the basis of what came to be known as the 'scheduling' of ancient monuments. Although inhabited houses were specifically excluded, apart from those that were only occupied by caretakers, a high proportion of castles that (incidentally) were likely to be seen as candidates for restoration, or that were in need of conservation, were progressively added to the list of scheduled monuments.

Initially, the only controls over works at monuments came from a clause in the Act which said that owners had to give one month's notice of their intentions to carry out works. If the government wished to intervene in those proposed works, it was necessary to go through the cumbersome process of seeking a preservation order, which then had to be confirmed by parliament within a period of eighteen months. This situation was eventually changed in 1979 by the Ancient Monuments and Archaeological Areas Act, which required owners to apply for scheduled monument consent for all works that might have a physical impact on scheduled monuments. As a result of this change, consent had to be given before work could proceed, and under present arrangements the process of considering applications for scheduled monument consent by Scottish Ministers is dealt with by Historic Scotland.

In addition to being scheduled, many ruined castles and tower houses are listed as historic buildings under the Planning (Listed Buildings and Conservation

Areas) (Scotland) Act of 1997, and in the case of listing it is possible to grade them according to their national or more local significance. But in cases of dual designation, it is the scheduled status that takes precedence, since ancient monuments legislation was first enacted as early as 1882, whereas Historic Buildings legislation dates back to 1945. There is the further possibility of roofless castles and tower houses being listed though not scheduled. In those cases, any works that might affect the character of the building require listed building consent, and application for this has to be made to the local planning authority.

So far as scheduled monuments are concerned, the assumption that lay behind the original legislation was that, since they were being designated as monuments because of the value of the architectural, archaeological and historical evidence they embodied, they should as far as possible be preserved for future generations without further change. Nevertheless, it has generally been recognised in Scotland that, except in the case of castles of the greatest significance or of those that have a particular importance as ruins in their landscape setting, sympathetic restoration for a renewed use may be an appropriate way of securing their future. This has been seen as most likely to be an acceptable approach for at least some of those abandoned tower houses for which there is little prospect of other ways being found of ensuring their continued preservation. As a result there have been few cases where the legislation has been used to prevent restoration from taking place, and the powers provided by the legislation have in the majority of cases been used with the aim of ensuring that works of this kind are carried out in the most sensitive manner, rather than in order to prevent them taking place.

Initially, the help that could be offered to an owner who wished to restore a castle was limited to practical advice. In 1953, however, the Historic Buildings and Ancient Monuments Act made it possible to offer 'grants for the purpose of defraying in whole or in part any expenditure incurred or to be incurred in the repair or maintenance of a building appearing to the Minister to be of outstanding historic or architectural interest'. Although funds provided through taxation have necessarily always been limited, and can only be offered to buildings of outstanding quality, the help that has been provided through grant assistance in aiding restoration or conservation will become evident in the discussion of many of the cases considered in the following chapters. These grants, which are now dealt with at first hand by Historic Scotland, were initially administered by a newly established Historic Buildings Council for Scotland, and almost from the beginning financial support was being offered towards the restoration of derelict or ruined tower houses, with the semi-derelict Pitheavlis (Perthshire) being one of the first to receive financial assistance in 1954.

In a contribution to a collection of papers on castle restoration published by Robert Clow in 2000, David Walker, a previous Chief Inspector of Historic Buildings (who has also contributed the final chapter to this book), drew a number of fascinating conclusions about what had been achieved through state grant assistance to castle restoration projects. A review that he had undertaken in 1985 had shown that, as might be expected, the most successful operations had been carried out at castles that had been relatively complete; indeed of 53 abandoned castles whose restoration had been assisted by grants, 35 had retained their roofs. Castles in that state are generally less problematic to restore because there are fewer difficulties in establishing the details of their historic state, and their restoration also tends to be less expensive since they call for relatively little reinstatement of worked masonry. Professor Walker also suggested that, apart from more recent financial constraints, one of the reasons that there have been fewer restorations in recent years is that 'the best-preserved, best-located and most readily available subjects for restoration had already been undertaken'. That is not to say that there are no longer any castles that might be seen as candidates for restoration, though many of the remaining potential candidates are likely to require greater resources on the part of those undertaking the work as a result of the loss of significant parts of their historic fabric. They may also entail greater challenges if there is inadequate physical, archaeological or pictorial evidence for their missing parts.

Grants from the Historic Buildings Council were usually limited to works aimed at bringing a historic structure back into some form of active use. However, as it came to be appreciated that there were many 'monuments' that were unlikely to be brought back into active use, and that could never be offered the protection of state care, it was accepted that other forms of funding should be made available. In 1979 a new Ancient Monuments Act made it possible for government 'to undertake, or assist in, or defray or contribute towards the cost of the preservation, maintenance and management of any ancient monument'. Since then, as will be seen from several of the cases discussed in Section Two below, a significant proportion of the allocation of ancient monument grants has been dedicated to the stabilisation and consolidation of roofless castles, providing a parallel stream of funding to that available for restoration.

Some cases of the removal of later additions

One final point that should perhaps be made in this chapter is that ways of life and social expectations continue to change, and this can sometimes mean that what were thought of as permanent solutions to dealing with castles in the past have not always proved to be as permanent as expected. This is seen particularly clearly in the case of some of those castles that were greatly augmented around a historic core in the course of the 19th century, but whose resultant great size has made them difficult to occupy in changed times. Many of these enlargements were undertaken in order to accommodate large house parties in considerable luxury, and they depended on a complex hierarchy of relatively poorly paid servants to run them efficiently. However, very few owners of great houses can now afford to entertain so lavishly, even if they wished to do so, and those who could afford such hospitality would be hard pressed to find sufficient numbers of servants to make it feasible. This has left many great mansions that have a castle at their heart with a rather uncertain future. While some have lent themselves to forms of public or institutional use, including adaptation as hotels and schools, even those uses have not always proved viable in the longer term, and numbers of augmented castles now have a precarious twilight existence as decaying or roofless shells.

In some cases, an attempt has been made to reduce them to more manageable proportions so that they can continue to be used or lived in, or simply in the hope that by doing this a suitable use will eventually be found. An example of the former approach may be seen at Duntreath (Stirlingshire). There, after a period of having been abandoned, the tower house and associated buildings had been enormously extended by Charles Wilson and David Thomson in 1856, and again by Sydney Mitchell in the years around 1890. But by the years after the Second World War a great house of the kind that had resulted was no longer easily manageable, and in 1958 much of the 19th-century work was demolished in order to make it more easily habitable to modern standards. A partly related process may be seen at Hoddom (Dumfriesshire), one of the castles that has been touched on above (Fig 3.11). In that case, a considerable portion of the 19th-century additions was progressively demolished between 1953 and 1975, and parts of what remains now serve the caravan park that has been established in the castle's policies, while other parts await an appropriate use.

One lesson that should perhaps be drawn from such cases is that, since approaches to dealing with castles may have a finite life expectancy, it is important to ensure that nothing is done that might eventually leave the castle in a worse state than it was in before the work started.

Figure 3.11 Hoddom Castle, in its final state as a residence (© RCAHMS. SC 1203754, Licensor www.rcahms.gov.uk)

Section Two
Conserving Castles

CHAPTER 4

Introductory
comments

Although the principal theme of this book is the restoration of castles for renewed use, since the conservation of the existing fabric should always be the first practical stage in any process of restoration, it is hoped that it will be helpful to consider a number of cases in which castles have been conserved in their existing ruined state. It might be added that, because works of conservation generally stop at stabilisation and consolidation of the masonry fabric, conserved buildings are of particular interest for our present purposes for the way they allow historic architectural and archaeological details to remain more easily accessible. As a result those details can be referred to as a source of comparative material in working up proposals for works at other castles; in essence, they give the opportunity to see historic methods and processes of construction at least partly unpicked. Beyond that, conserved buildings can allow the practical processes of stabilisation and consolidation that are appropriate in both restoration and conservation projects to remain more readily visible for reference than tends to be the case when complete restoration is carried out. It might also be mentioned that there is specific relevance in such projects for a number of castles to be discussed later in this book, where part of the complex has been restored for use and other parts simply conserved, as at Melgund (Angus) (see Figs 20.1–20.4) and Monimail (Fife) (see Figs 22.1–22.2), and where there are thus elements of both conservation and restoration.

A leading aim in conservation works is that there should be minimal interference with the historic fabric, so that as far as possible all the evidence for the building's architectural history that is embodied within that fabric can be passed on to future generations without modification. Almost inevitably, however, where works are to be undertaken at buildings that are exposed to the unforgiving elements, and particularly when those buildings have lost both the wall-head protection of their roofs and the bracing once provided by their floors, measures have to be taken to introduce an adequate level of new strength. All of this requires the most careful consideration if there is to be no detraction from the essential character of the building, and this is especially the case in buildings that have come to be regarded as objects of great beauty in their ruined state and within their landscape setting, as at Ardvreck (Sutherland) (see Fig 8.1). In such cases there is the additional challenge of preserving a unique and site-specific aesthetic quality, as well as of avoiding a potentially sterile sense that the building has somehow been simply 'preserved in aspic'. It must be stressed that there can be no single 'correct' body of solutions, and unfortunately it is almost invariably the case that, whatever solutions are adopted, there will be some negative impact. One of the skills of those involved in work of this kind lies in choosing a course that protects the character of the castle, together with the evidence it embodies, as completely as possible, and that is as fully in sympathy with its essential spirit as can be achieved.

On that basis, the particular needs of each site have to be carefully assessed on their own terms, though there are a number of basic principles that it is best to take into account in seeking a way forward. Amongst these are the aspiration that, as far as possible, nothing should be done that could not be undone at a later stage if it proved not to have been in the building's best interests. It should also be borne in mind that very few buildings are the product of a single principal phase of construction, and the most extreme case considered in this book which illustrates that is Hume (Berwickshire), which is now as much an 18th-century eye-catcher as a medieval castle (see Figs 6.1–6.2). At Hume it was accepted from the start of the conservation works that the later phases of construction were as deserving of respect and retention as the original building, since they are as much a part of its history as what was first built. Underlying everything else, however, should be an acceptance of the need to understand the structure and history of the building as fully as possible if the right decisions are to be reached.

The conservation projects to be briefly considered in this second section of the book consist mainly of cases where the owners, whether individuals or public bodies, have decided that something must be done to prevent the further decay of a ruined castle in their ownership or stewardship, and have then set about trying to bring together funding that will allow this to be put into effect. It would be misleading not to make clear from the start that funding can be a major problem in projects of this kind, since the work is highly labour intensive and demands advanced levels of craftsmanship combined with specialist professional supervisory skills. There can be the additional problem that a number of the sites, including most notably Ardvreck, are very remote, and there are consequent problems of bringing together teams of sufficiently skilled craftsmen and of transporting materials. Nevertheless, however daunting the costs might be, where the castle is of a sufficiently high level of significance, there may be a range of sources of funding worth exploring. It will be seen, for example, that in all of the cases discussed in this book, despite the fact that the funds available for this purpose are very limited, Historic Scotland has been able to provide significant levels of support through its grants programme.

Once possible sources of funding have been identified, a first problem that has to be confronted in planning a conservation project is that of determining how much should be carried out. At Cessford (Roxburghshire) (see Figs 9.1–9.3), it was decided that nothing should be done beyond the works that were considered necessary to deal with those structural problems that were placing the stability of the building at greatest risk. In following this approach, however, it was accepted that further works at a future date are likely to be in the castle's best interests if funds can be found. It is a mistake, however, to imagine that it could ever be possible to make a building secure for all time, and it is usually best if conservation is planned to leave a building in a stable state for a period of no more than a number of decades. The consequences can be very damaging if this is not accepted. This may be seen with stark clarity at a number of castles where works were carried out between the 1930s and 1970s, including many of those in state care, where for the most laudable of motives the masonry joints were painstakingly raked out and repointed in hard cement, which it was assumed would have a very long life expectancy. Unfortunately, it is now clear that at a high proportion of the buildings treated in this way that approach is resulting in damaging erosion of the stonework, and the problem is exacerbated because the risks of damage likely to be caused in removing cement pointing can sometimes be as great as those of leaving it in place. In general, it is now accepted that it is best to rely on materials that are as similar as possible to those employed when the castle was first built. This usually means using lime mortar that replicates the characteristics of the mortar originally used in the part of the building to be treated, based on analysis of that mortar, combined with stone of the same geological type as that first used. At the same time, while ensuring that the new work is both physically and visually sympathetic with the historic fabric, ways should be found of making that new work identifiable on close inspection if additional problems are not to be created for those who will wish to understand these buildings and their structural history in the future.

Amongst the cases considered in the following chapters, some of the problems resulting from the previous use of an intractable modern material were to be seen at Drumin (Moray) (see Fig 7.1) where, as was done in many other cases, the exposed wall heads had been thickly coated with cement, which it was assumed would prevent water penetrating into the wall core virtually indefinitely. However, such an inert crust cannot respond to the natural movement of a building, and it almost invariably cracks, allowing water to enter the wall and, even more damagingly, permitting saplings to take hold, whose roots can then penetrate deep into the masonry. When wall heads now have to be protected, depending on the particular circumstances of the site and the nature of the fabric, it is sometimes felt preferable to follow the course that nature itself tends to foster, by introducing a thick coat of turf, a finish often referred to as 'soft topping'. In fact this is by no means a new approach, since we know it was being applied at Ardvreck as early as 1862. It is, however, an approach that is generally only appropriate where the walls are of sufficient thickness for the turf to become firmly bedded into the rubble core, and where the site is not subject to high levels of wind erosion. At Cessford it was possible for parts of the naturally formed turf cap to the walls simply to be retained in place, while in areas that showed some evidence of distress the turf was removed and then replaced once the underlying masonry had been consolidated (Fig 4.1). At Drumin, and in the roofless parts of Melgund, the walls were carefully conserved before turf was set in place (see Fig 20.1). One potential problem with turf as a wall topping that has to be guarded against is that it can provide fertile ground for woody growth, in the form of either saplings or ivy. Such growth should never be allowed to become

Figure 4.1 Cessford Castle, the 'soft topping' along the exposed wall head

established, since penetrating roots can cause great damage to masonry, and it should always be remembered that, as with any building, periodic maintenance must be an ongoing commitment.

In addition to using historically appropriate materials, it is increasingly accepted in works of conservation that traditional techniques of construction which reflect those originally employed should be used as far as possible. Nevertheless, there can be cases where it is less damaging to the historic fabric to use modern engineering techniques, especially in situations where the modern insertions will not be visually intrusive. Amongst the cases considered in this book a variety of such approaches have been adopted for parts of Ardvreck, Cessford and Invergarry (Inverness-shire) (see Fig 10.3). At Cessford it had been expected that the need to deal with a number of major fissures resulting from structural movement would require the insertion of several stainless steel tie rods and anchors, some of which were expected to be highly visible. In the event it was found possible to reduce the number required, and to conceal most of them within the masonry. The fissures themselves were filled in with new masonry that was set back a short distance from the wall face, so that the visual integrity of the masonry was maintained, while still making clear the extent of what has been done for those in the future who might wish to understand the castle's more recent history.

In planning conservation works it is essential that full account is taken of the archaeology that both underlies the building and exists within its fabric. In essence this means that, wherever ground surfaces or historic fabric are to be disturbed, the work should be supervised and recorded by either a specialist archaeologist or an architectural historian, and in some cases by both. This requirement may be less in cases of conservation than in restoration projects, since services such as electricity, water and drainage usually do not have to be brought in and out of a building that is not being put to some form of new use. Nevertheless, where there is an overburden of earth and collapsed masonry above historic ground and floor levels that has to be lowered, there will certainly be a requirement for archaeological input. At Cessford, after careful consideration of the options, it was decided that there was no compelling need to cut into ground levels or internal overburdens, and the principal archaeological requirement was thus to record and interpret the evidence that was found within the fabric. Where archaeological investigation is to be undertaken, it should be remembered that such operations are by their very nature unpredictable, and there is no way of knowing in advance how informative it will be. At Drumin, where archaeologically supervised excavation was carried out in advance of work on the masonry fabric, it was found that any evidence relating to the periods when the castle had been occupied had already been destroyed as a result of horticultural activity. This is relatively unusual, however, and of the cases discussed in this book, important evidence for destroyed parts of the castle has been found in the course of archaeological investigations at Balgonie, Melgund, Monimail and Mugdock (Stirlingshire), amongst others.

When a castle has been conserved there is generally a wish to make it more accessible for visitors, and ways have to be found of doing this that meet public safety requirements without introducing excessively intrusive new features. At Mugdock there was already a system of medieval stairways that permitted access to the wall head of the most complete of the towers, and that could be safely used by the public once the work was complete. But there can sometimes be a temptation to find ways of affording access to areas which would certainly be rewarding for visitors to reach, yet which could only be achieved through the insertion of visually unsympathetic stairs and platforms. At Drumin, for example, there was a natural wish to allow visitors access to the upper parts of the tower, from where they would be able to enjoy fine views across the surrounding countryside. It was found, however, that the only means of achieving this would be by the installation of a system of stairs and platforms that would detract from the appearance of the castle itself, and that would also be extremely costly to maintain. In that case it was eventually decided to do no more than create a viewing platform at first-floor level, on the upper surface of the consolidated and water-proofed vault.

It should also be mentioned here that something which may be lost sight of in planning for visitor access is that increased pedestrian traffic can result in damage to the building and its setting. At Ardvreck, for example, greater access to this beautiful site has resulted in damage to some of the parts that have recently been conserved, and in such cases there may be a need to find means of managing the ways by which visitors are encouraged to make their way around the building without having to clamber over the masonry itself.

Having considered some of the factors involved in the conservation of castles, we shall now move on to outline a number of individual cases where this has been achieved in a range of ways.

CHAPTER 5

Mugdock Castle

From at least the mid-13th century the lands of Mugdock were a possession of the Graham family, and the barony of Mugdock, created in 1458, is still one of the titles of the Dukes of Montrose. The site of the medieval castle is a plateau overlooking the south-west corner of Mugdock Loch, Strathblane, Stirlingshire (Fig 1.1; Fig 5.1), although in its first form no more than a part of the southern side of the plateau was occupied by the castle. A sequence of later houses on the site was built over the eastern portion of the castle, though it is not clear if that portion was demolished to make way for the new buildings, or if those parts of the castle had already collapsed by the time the later houses were built. On the evidence of what survives, it appears likely that the castle's original plan consisted of a roughly quadrangular courtyard with square towers at the four corners, and with a gatehouse projected forwards at the centre of the south wall. In this it invites comparison with sites such as the episcopal castle at St Andrews (Fife), as rebuilt by Bishop Walter Trail in the years around 1400, though there is an even longer tradition of this kind of layout, as perhaps seen at Panmure Castle (Angus).

Figure 5.1 Mugdock Castle, an aerial view (© RCAHMS. SC 1203756, Licensor www.rcahms.gov.uk)

Figure 5.2 Mugdock Castle, the south-west tower

Of the castle's presumed four towers, that at the south-west corner stands virtually to its full height (Fig 5.2). The ground floor of that tower, which is provided with a latrine, did not have any internal communication with the upper floors; the main entrance to the tower, which is at first-floor level, is now approached by a largely modern forestair, and from that level upwards there is first a spiral stair and then straight flights. Between the first and second floors there are external changes in the alignment of three of the walls at the point where they appear to have risen clear of the curtain wall, and this corresponds with the slightly awkwardly contrived internal change from a spiral stair to a straight flight. Together these suggest a break in the building operation and the completion of the tower to a changed design. The upper floors have retained a number of details that together point to a date in the earlier 14th century for the completion of the tower: over the first floor is a ribbed barrel vault, while, more significantly, at third-floor level are small ogee-headed windows and a doorway with a shouldered lintel.

The north-west tower, which is both larger in plan and more thinly walled than its south-western neighbour, survives only for a single storey, and that lowest level is now covered by a barrel vault that was inserted at some later stage. The two towers are connected by a length of curtain wall, within which there is a gateway, and there are traces of other buildings that would have abutted it. There is a further length of curtain wall to the east of the south-west tower; this terminates against the west flank of the main gatehouse, within which are to be seen the slots for a portcullis.

In the 15th century the castle was extended to encompass the whole of the plateau, and a new gate arch was constructed to the west of the original complex. A variety of structures was progressively added against the new perimeter wall and within the enclosed area. The best-preserved stretch of the wall runs westward from the south-west tower of the first castle, and along its inner wall is the shell of a well-preserved domestic range datable to the 16th and 17th centuries (Fig 5.3), against which two forestairs led up to its first floor. Slighter traces of the perimeter wall are to be found along the west and parts of the east side of the enlarged courtyard, and outside the greater part of this enclosure a ditch has been cut. At the northernmost part of the courtyard is a rectangular building whose east–west alignment has suggested that it had been built as a chapel; there is also a tradition that a holy water stoup once existed in its south wall. However, the partial survival of a contiguous latrine projection may indicate that the building was intended to serve a secular function.

The castle continued in use as a residence for the head of the Graham family into the 18th century, and the second Marquess of Montrose built a new house on the east side of the site in 1655. It was probably only after the first Duke of Montrose had built a fine mansion at Buchanan, in c 1724, that Mugdock came to be less favoured as a primary residence, though repairs are known to have been carried out at various dates in the 18th century, and a terraced walled garden was formed on the slope between the castle and loch around the 1820s. There was a revival in the castle's fortunes in 1875, when a substantial residence designed in the baronial style by the architect James Sellars was built for a new tenant, J Guthrie Smith (Fig 5.4). This overlooked the terraced gardens and loch, and probably incorporated parts of the house of 1655. It was connected to the south-west tower of the castle by a stone bridge supporting a half-timbered corridor, and the interior of that tower was partly refitted at the same time. Extensive ancillary buildings for this house were constructed to the west of the earlier castle, within the extended 15th-century enclosure.

In 1945 the castle and surrounding parkland were sold by the Duke of Montrose to Sir Hugh Fraser, and some years later Sir Hugh was exploring the possibility of conserving the medieval castle. However, the costs proved to be prohibitive at that time, particularly since by then the condition of the castle was deteriorating. The process of deterioration was greatly exacerbated by a fire in 1965 that gutted much of the 19th-century house, with further damage being

Figure 5.3 Mugdock Castle, the domestic range

RENEWED LIFE FOR SCOTTISH CASTLES

Figure 5.4 Mugdock Castle, the later house (© RCAHMS. SC 1203650, Licensor www.rcahms.gov.uk)

caused during the filming of a television series called *The Borderers*. In 1967 Sir Hugh offered the castle into state care, but, although it was to be scheduled as a monument of national importance two years later, the costs involved meant that state guardianship was not a viable option. He also offered it to the National Trust for Scotland in 1968, though funding difficulties meant that offer could not be accepted either. Eventually, in 1981 Sir Hugh offered the castle and park to Central Regional Council, together with a small endowment, and the council had the vision to see that both the park and the castle could be a great asset for the people of the region. Over the next few years a way forward was progressively put together with funding from a number of bodies, including substantial grant assistance from Historic Scotland.

So far as the castle was concerned, in 1984 Geoffrey Jarvis, of Boys Jarvis Architects, was appointed to prepare a programme of works. The initial proposals were to conserve the historic fabric of the castle, to reroof the south-west tower, and to restore the 16th-century west range as a visitor centre and a caretaker's house. The works were therefore intended to embrace elements of both conservation and restoration. It was also initially proposed to demolish what remained of the 19th-century house and its ancillary buildings, though Historic Scotland persuaded the council that the house should be regarded as representing a significant part of the historical development of the site and should therefore be retained. The work was initiated on that basis.

The work involved a certain amount of archaeological excavation. In 1986 the line of the north wall of the first courtyard was located at the point where it joined the north-west tower. Within that tower, as part of the process of water-proofing the barrel vault that had been inserted within it, evidence was found for the fireplace and slop drain of the kitchen that had been installed at first-floor level.

In the earlier stages of the project, one of the more common tensions entailed in work of this kind emerged. It became clear that a highly skilled mason, whose training naturally led him to assume that every effort should be made to introduce fresh strength into the fabric, was doing this in a way that was to some extent in conflict with the need to preserve the historic evidence within that fabric. In the 16th-century west range, where some of the window embrasures were bridged by timber safe lintels, the mason was found to have replaced the safe lintels of one window with a stone rear arch. Safe lintels are, of course, an inherently weak form of construction, and in the contract for Holyrood Palace of 1672, for example, they were expressly forbidden; they are an even greater problem in a building that is open to the elements, as at Mugdock. It is therefore easy to understand why a practical mason might think it appropriate to replace them. Nevertheless, in a building that had been constructed with both rear arches and safe lintels in different parts, the two forms of construction are an important indicator of the building sequence and the inter-relationship between parts. In such cases it is particularly important that ways should be found of either retaining the original timbers, or of replacing them on a like-for-like basis and making clear that they are replacements. This highlighted the need to ensure that, in addition to employing craftsmen of a high calibre, those craftsmen must be encouraged to understand the need to avoid disturbing significant evidence.

The project represented a major commitment on the part of Central Region and its successor, Stirling Council, at a time when there were many other calls on its funds, and it should not perhaps be a matter of surprise that there was a stage when the work lost some momentum. In 1987, a fresh initiative was established, however, and, following the appointment of Thom Pollock of Cadell Architects (later of Pollock Hammond Architects), the remaining necessary works were freshly costed and phased. The final stage was completed in 2002–03, by which time Historic Scotland had given some £127,000 in grant assistance, representing about one-third of the costs of consolidation of the historic fabric. Most of what was initially envisaged had been achieved and, though it has not so far been possible to establish a visitor centre and caretaker's house in the west range, that range has been fully stabilised.

The castle and park remain in the ownership of Stirling Council, but they are managed on Stirling's behalf by East Dunbartonshire Council, which has a 50-year lease, and has provided a resident manager and ranger service in the park. The park is proving to be a much-used resource, attracting the loyal support of many volunteers, and there is a visitor centre adjacent to the shell of Craigend House. The castle itself is carefully maintained, and is accessible to visitors throughout the year, with information boards providing a good level of information. Displays illustrating the history of the castle and its owners have been installed in the south-west tower and the stump of the north-west tower, and in the summer months they are opened to the public for a small charge which pays for much of the low-level ongoing maintenance required. The power required for visitor access and to light the displays is supplied by means of solar panels that have been located on the south pitch of the restored roof over the south-west tower, behind the wall-head parapet. Although there had been some concern that these solar panels would be intrusively visible, and their upper parts can indeed be seen from certain vantage points within the park, on balance their visual impact is relatively slight. The present state of the castle reflects considerable credit on Central Regional Council, Stirling Council and East Dunbartonshire Council, and demonstrates what can be achieved at a site of this kind.

CHAPTER 6

Hume Castle

The first and most lasting impression offered by Hume Castle, Berwickshire, is that of a prominent eye-catcher created on the whim of a romantic 18th-century landowner, but in fact it is a building that has a great deal of historical and architectural interest (Fig 1.2; Fig 6.1).

The castle was associated with the Home, or Hume, family for many centuries, following a grant of the lands to William of Hume shortly before 1214. It appears to have been the land that gave the name to the family, rather than the family to the castle, and it has been suggested that such a naturally strong rock outcrop may have been fortified before the grant to William, though it would be difficult to identify positively any masonry that could be so early. The most prominent element of the castle was a curtain wall defining an approximately quadrangular enclosure, so far as the irregular contours of the site would allow. The curtain wall would have provided protection for ranges of domestic buildings and offices around its inner faces, though little more than an enigmatic central mass of

Figure 6.1 Hume Castle

masonry now stands above ground. There would probably have been outer courtyards on the rock terraces on each side of the main enclosure.

Plans of the type seen in the surviving core at Hume are now most commonly found in the northern and western Highland areas, as at Mingary (Argyll) or in a more highly developed form at Dunstaffnage (Argyll) (see Fig 1.3). Hume gains an added interest from being one of the few examples of the type outside that area. Its existence could raise the tantalising possibility that there were others in the south-east that did not survive Robert I's policy of destroying strongholds that might be held against him by the English. It should be added that Hume appears to have formed the first stage in a chain of beacon stances intended to give warning of the approach of English troops.

Alexander Hume was created a lord of parliament in 1473, and, as the family's fortunes advanced, it is likely the castle was modified on a number of occasions. A shot hole of vertical dumb-bell form in the west wall points to works being carried out around the later 15th century, for example. If credence can be given to the tradition that Queen Mary of Gueldres was staying at the castle in 1460 when James II was killed at the siege of Roxburgh, it would suggest that the accommodation afforded within the castle was of a high order.

Most of the firm information we have on the castle dates from the 16th and 17th centuries, and relates to its defence from, or by, English forces. In the course of the Duke of Somerset's invasion of Scotland in 1547, Hume was taken as one of three English bases; although earlier fortified by French forces, it had been quickly surrendered to Somerset. Large sums were subsequently spent on strengthening the fortifications, in which the surveyor William Ridgeway was involved. But by 1549 it had been retaken by Lord Hume, and in 1550 captured English artillery was being stored within it.

In 1650 the castle figured in the resistance against Cromwell's parliamentary army, leading to Thomas Cockburn's reputed defiant response to Colonel Fenwick:

> I William of the Wastle
> Am now in my castle
> And aw the dogs in the town
> Shan't gar me gang down.

By that stage it is doubtful if the Hume family regarded the castle as a viable residence, particularly since in 1604 the family had been granted an earldom. However, the head of a collateral branch of the family, the Earl of Marchmont, who had high ambitions for his side of the family, began to take a different form of interest in the castle 150 years later. In 1750–54 the third earl was building a splendid new house to the designs of Thomas Gibson at Marchmont, about 5 miles to the north-west of Home. The castle was prominently visible in views from his estate, which was being landscaped on the advice of William Adam, and this presented him with the opportunity both to make the castle into a fine landscape feature and to stress the ancestry of his family in doing so. It is not known either when the earl acquired the castle, or when he rebuilt its upper

Figure 6.2 Hume Castle, as depicted by Francis Grose in 1789

walls to give it even greater prominence as an eye-catcher when viewed from a distance, though it is attractive to suspect that it was around the time that his son was granted the title of Lord Hume in 1776. The astonishingly over-scaled battlements that were added to the wall head were certainly complete before 1789, when Francis Grose published an engraving of the castle (Fig 6.2). Tragically, the third earl's dynastic ambitions foundered on the premature death of his son in 1781, and on his own death in 1794 Marchmont passed to Sir William Purves.

So far as can be judged from what is now to be seen, in carrying out his work on the castle Lord Marchmont retained whatever walling still stood secure, and we must therefore be grateful to him for preserving the remains of what is on any assessment a highly significant castle. It hardly needs stating that his addition of oversized wall-head crenellation is something that would no longer be seen as acceptable and, indeed, it is something that is unlikely even to be suggested today. Nevertheless, it has given an added dimension of interest for modern viewers by offering a relatively early example of the romantic exploitation of a medieval building as part of the wider landscaped setting of a great house.

In 1929 Hume, with the lands around it, was acquired by the state for land settlement. The acquisition of the castle was no more than an incidental consequence of the purchase of the land, however; there was never any intention of carrying out work on the castle, and no funds were available for that purpose. As a consequence, by the 1950s it was in a structurally fragile state and had been closed to the public. In 1955 the National Trust for Scotland was asked if it might be prepared to accept the castle, and the Trust in turn asked the Ministry of Works if it could do so. Neither body had the funds to be able to consider taking it on at that time; nevertheless, in 1963 its significance was recognised when it was scheduled as a monument of national importance.

The question of what should be done for the castle assumed greater urgency towards the end of 1969, when the Department of Agriculture and Fisheries decided that it should sell the land, and the castle along with it. The land was eventually put up for sale in 1972, though there was still no clear way forward for the castle, and in the following year the works that would be necessary to stabilise it were costed at £11,000, with a further £3000 for desirable works; these figures were later adjusted to £6000 and £5000 respectively. As discussions continued, the anticipated cost of works escalated alarmingly, and by 1981 it was suggested that essential consolidation could cost about £75,000, with possible total costs reaching as much as £400,000.

By 1984 the land had been sold, but the castle had been held back from the sale and was the only part that remained in the ownership of the Department of Agriculture and Fisheries. Following further discussions, it was agreed in 1988 that the most appropriate way forward would be for the castle to remain in the ownership of the Secretary of State for Scotland for the time being, but that a lease on it should be granted to the Berwickshire Civic Society, which had expressed a willingness to act as an umbrella body. The necessary repairs to the castle were to be paid for through ancient monuments grants, and a programme of works was drawn up by the architect David Mylne, aimed at placing the castle in a structurally stable condition through straightforward consolidation of the masonry, and with no restoration of missing features. Hume presented rather different problems from many projects of this kind, since there was probably almost as much fabric dating from the 18th century as from the Middle Ages, and it was by no means always clear what dated from when. However, an underlying principle in such work should generally be that all phases of the building's history are fully respected as making a valid contribution to its current state, and this principle was of particular significance at Hume, where its remodelling as an 18th-century eye-catcher is a fascinating part of the story it has to tell.

The works were planned to run in three phases from 1989 to 1991, following preparatory operations in 1988, and were expected to cost £126,500. The initial intention was that the work should be carried out as an Employment Training Scheme of the Manpower Services Commission, though this did not prove possible in the event, with an inevitable consequence for costs. By the time work was completed in 1992, £135,954.05 had been paid in grants. It was then agreed that the relatively small running costs should be met through annual payments under a management agreement between Historic Scotland and the Berwickshire Civic Society. As a final point it may be mentioned that, since the completion of the work, ownership of the castle has passed to the Hume Castle Preservation Trust, which is sponsored by the Clan Hume Society.

CHAPTER 7

Drumin Castle

Drumin Castle, Moray, which was the main residence of the barony of Inveravon, is located on a promontory at the point where the Rivers Avon (pronounced A'an) and Livet join (Fig 1.3). The site commands views of these glens and once dominated the approach along them toward Speyside.

Little is know of the castle's history and the exact date of construction is not recorded. King Robert II granted the lands of Badenoch and Strathavon (including Drumin) to his son, Alexander Stewart, in the early 1370s and it is thought that the castle may have been built for that son, who came to be known as the Wolf of Badenoch as a result of his predatory behaviour. His grandson, Sir Walter Stewart, sold the estate to Alexander Gordon, third Earl of Huntly, in 1490. The earl did not reside at Drumin, however, his main residences being Huntly Castle and Bog o' Gight. Rather it was his son, Alexander Gordon, and then from 1546 the Grants of Freuchie, who managed the Gordon family's affairs in Badenoch and Strathavon, who lived there. From the late 16th century, the earl's residence in Strathavon was at the newly built Blairfindy Castle at nearby Glenlivet. Subsequently Drumin Castle is believed to have been occupied by various members of the Stewart family as tenants; Charles Stewart of Drumin is thought to have been the last resident of the castle, and it is presumed to have fallen into disuse around the mid-18th century.

The tower, which was of rectangular plan, is aligned from north-west to south-east, with rubble-built walls that are nearly 3m thick at the base. The north-west wall survives almost to full height (Fig 7.1), as does the north-east wall for much of its length, but the greater part of the south-west wall has collapsed, as has the whole of the south-east wall. It is likely that one cause of the collapse was that the south-east wall contained the entrance and the stair to the upper floors, and was thus less solidly built than the other walls. The ground floor of the tower was covered by a barrel vault, above which were three further floors, all provided with fireplaces; there was presumably also a garret storey within the roof space, though nothing remains of the gables that would have contained the roof. At the wall head there are fragmentary remains of the corbelling that supported a parapet along the outer face of a wall walk (Fig 7.1), and there may also have been corner rounds and a machicolation.

In 1818–19 a new house (the present farmhouse) was built at Drumin for William Mitchell, the factor to the Duke of Gordon. It is likely that much of the stone for this house and the associated buildings was taken from the collapsed and dismantled parts of the tower. In the later 19th or early 20th century the ruined tower appears to have been used as a store, probably associated with the garden

Figure 7.1 Drumin
Castle

of the house, which entailed the creation of a lean-to structure at the south-east
end of the tower. This consisted of two small rooms separated by an entrance gap
closed by an iron gate leading to the rest of the cellar. These rooms, along with
the entrance and the broken edge of the vault, were covered with a single pitched
roof. It was perhaps at the same time that the tower was first consolidated, with
the south-west wall being extended to form a buttress incorporating a straight
stair giving access to the first-floor hall. These works, and the ivy-strewn nature
of the ruin as depicted soon afterwards, suggest that efforts were being made to
adapt the tower as a Romantic garden feature for the house.

The Glenlivet Estate, including Drumin Castle, was purchased by the Crown
Estate in 1937, and in 1947 the Ministry of Works agreed to assume responsibility
for Drumin, Blairfindy and Auchindoun castles. It may have been during the
time that the castle was in state care that the wall heads were capped in concrete
and the top of the vault tanked, also with concrete. However, in 1957 the Ancient
Monuments Board decided that Blairfindy and Drumin were not of sufficiently
high significance to be in state care, and there were also issues of providing public
access to Drumin through the garden of a private residence. As a result the
guardianship agreement was revoked but, since it was still regarded as being of
national importance, it was designated as a scheduled monument in 1963.

In 1992, the Crown Estate, through its agents Smiths Gore, contacted Historic
Scotland to discuss repair work to the tower and the possibility of grant
assistance. It was noted at the time that its condition was causing concern, with
ivy obscuring much of the masonry. The safety concerns were such that in
1993 a post and wire fence was erected around the tower under archaeological
supervision. However, nothing of archaeological significance was found at that

time, and in fact it was noted that the area around the tower appeared to have been cultivated to a considerable depth over many years, suggesting that survival of archaeological evidence was unlikely.

In 1993 a Historic Scotland architect's advisory report was prepared, and in the following year the Forres office of Law and Dunbar-Nasmith Architects was appointed by the Crown Estate to lead the project. In 1996 preliminary works began on site once scheduled monument consent had been granted. The works included scaffolding the underside of the vault to allow initial vegetation removal, and archaeological investigation of overburdens, both in the vaulted cellar and on the top of the vault. Other scaffolding was erected to allow survey work to be carried out as part of preparing a scheme of works. The excavations confirmed that there were no significant archaeological deposits dating from the occupation of the tower in the medieval period; all deposits related to the 19th- and early 20th-century use of the castle. The archaeological work, which was carried out by the Centre for Field Archaeology (CFA), was supported by a grant of £4176 from Historic Scotland.

Figure 7.2 Drumin Castle, work in progress

Due to the costs involved, it was decided that the consolidation works should themselves be phased over three years, with grants totalling over £107,000 to be made by Historic Scotland. In 1999 the contract for the stabilisation of the masonry was awarded to Cumming and Co, and in 2000 the first major phase of works began with the consolidation of the wall heads, together with the repointing of the west external elevation and works to stabilise openings in the east elevation. The wall head had previously been capped by a layer of cementitious concrete and a profusion of saplings and small shrubs were growing through cracks which had developed. When removed, it was found that on the west and north elevations the wall head was better preserved beneath the capping than had been anticipated, with many of the original saddle stones and troughs of the wall-head wall walk surviving. By contrast the east elevation wall head was less well preserved and only a single trough survived. The decision had been made to 'soft-top' the wall heads to avoid the problems of a solid capping cracking and allowing water into the core of the wall; after consolidating the masonry the wall heads were therefore packed with puddled clay, onto which a layer of turf was applied (Fig 7.2).

Another significant issue that had to be tackled in the final phase of the project was how to treat the exposed upper surface of the vault. The cement screed, which may have been laid in the 1950s, was allowing water to percolate through the vault and was washing out the mortar. When this screed was broken up it was discovered that the haunch of the vault was filled with a build-up of soil which was holding moisture and which had allowed ivy to establish itself and proliferate. This material was removed and a gravel fill was introduced, on top of which sand and then lime concrete were laid. Taking in to account the very hard winter frosts that can be experienced at Drumin, it was decided that a lime concrete finish would not be robust enough to be left exposed and a top finish of a cement-based concrete was then laid, though this was carefully isolated from the surrounding masonry. It was designed to have a fall which would allow surface water to run to a gully and then beyond the walls of the castle.

Providing better access and interpretation had always been an aim of the project for the Crown Estate, but existing access to the castle was problematic since it was through a private garden. An answer was found by creating a new car park by the River Livet, with a path from there to the castle. The path works were carried out by the University of London Officer Training Corps as a Military Aid to the Civil Community project. In addition, there were discussions on the possibility of building an elevated viewing platform within the tower to allow access to second-floor level. This was not taken forward, but a timber balustrade was erected along the broken edge of the vault at first-floor level, allowing safe access to that level, and interpretive material on the castle's history and architecture has been provided. The castle was formally reopened by the Duke of York on 14 July 2005, at the conclusion of the project.

CHAPTER 8

Ardvreck Castle

Ardvreck Castle, which is a beautifully sited ruin on a promontory projecting from the north side of Loch Assynt in Sutherland (Fig 8.1), was the seat of the MacLeods of Assynt (Fig 1.4). On first sight the castle appears to be of the late 16th century, and, according to the *Statistical Account*, it bore the date 1591 or 1597, although other accounts give the date as 1581. However, research carried out as part of the recent conservation project has suggested two major building phases. The castle may have been first built by Angus Mor, third MacLeod of Assynt, in the second half of the 15th century, once the MacLeods had firmly established themselves in Assynt. In a second phase, in the late 16th century, the castle was enlarged, probably by Donald Ban, ninth MacLeod of Assynt; it was presumably these alterations that were recorded on the date stone referred to in the *Statistical Account* and that were shown in the sketch view on Pont's late 16th-century map.

As it was first built in the later 15th century, the main element of the castle is likely to have been a simple rectangular tower of three or four storeys. The late 16th-century alterations saw the addition of a round stair tower, which was corbelled out to the square at the upper levels. At the same time, the first-floor vault was inserted. The ground-floor vaulted chambers, which were accessed along a corridor whose outer wall was pierced with simple gun ports, are probably of similar date. These additions created a tower house that was in many ways characteristic of its time in northern Scotland, being comparable with Muckrach (Inverness-shire) or Birse (Aberdeenshire), though Ardvreck has unusual features due to its particular history and perhaps also to its distance from the main centres of castle building.

The south wall and the angle tower still stand to a considerable height, together with lengths of the east and west walls. The detailing is very simple, having been largely conditioned by the rubble masonry from which it is built, though the corbelling and the aperture surrounds (now largely robbed) were formed from imported sandstone. It is difficult to be certain of the original plan, but MacGibbon and Ross suggest that the main entrance was a doorway in the east wall at ground-floor level, immediately adjacent to the angle tower, which opened into the vaulted corridor running along the south side of the two barrel-vaulted chambers. A stair in the lower part of the angle tower led up to the first-floor hall, which was also eventually vaulted, and there may ultimately have been three further storeys above that. Access between the floors above the hall was by a smaller spiral stair that was corbelled out between the angle tower and the south wall. At a higher level the angle tower was transformed into a diagonally set cap house of square plan, with the salient angles carried

Figure 8.1 Ardvreck
Castle (Robin Noble)

on simple corbelling; the two storeys of chambers at that higher level are
each provided with a fireplace. The roof appears to have been covered with
stone slates.

The remains of a wall which crosses the neck of the promontory appears to
follow the line of an earlier rampart, along with a possibly water-filled ditch, all
of which augmented the promontory's natural defences. There are traces of other
buildings and a walled garden within the enclosed area, some of which probably
date from the period of the castle's occupation as a residence, while others,
including a barn and attached kiln, are of relatively late construction. These
features remind us that this limestone area was formerly more fertile than the
wild highland landscape of today might suggest.

The castle is now particularly remembered as being the place where the
Marquess of Montrose was briefly imprisoned by Neil MacLeod of Assynt after
his capture in 1650, and before his execution in Edinburgh. In 1672, the castle
was taken by the Mackenzies of Wester Ross following a siege; this, together
with a protracted legal dispute, ended the MacLeods possession of Ardvreck and
Assynt. In 1726, the Mackenzies built the nearby Calda House to replace the
old castle, but this was burnt down in 1737, in the course of a struggle between
the Earl of Seaforth and the Earl of Sutherland. Around 1760, Hugh MacLeod
of Geanies, a descendant of the MacLeods of Assynt, attempted to buy back

the estate, but was outbid by the Sutherland family. In 1795, the castle suffered further damage when it was struck by lightning. Two cannon, which some have suggested were from a wrecked Armada ship, were recorded as being at the castle as late as the 1960s.

The castle's importance was formally recognised in 1935 when it was scheduled. However, research by Malcolm Bangor-Jones has shown that interest in the preservation of the remains began much earlier than that. In 1862, George Birnie and Company, a Lochinver firm, was employed by the owner, the Duke of Sutherland, to repair the castle. The work consisted of 'upholding the remaining parts of the Ruin, by building up the breaches and rents, in walls, building up the snecks [pinnings] in face of walls, and Covering tops of ditto with Cement lime and turf, and covering Arches &c'. The total cost of the work was just over £63. The use of turf capping for the wall heads must be one of the earliest documented examples of that approach in a conservation project, and has resonances with the works carried out in the late 20th century. After the work was completed the tenant of Achmore sheep farm was given an annual allowance of £2 for one of his shepherds to look after the 'Old Castle of Ardvrack'. There are also indications that there were later phases of maintenance, as the round tower was at some stage roughly repointed with cement mortar.

Interest in the castle has tended to focus particularly on its scenic qualities and its romantic association with Montrose, and from the late 1950s there have been repeated calls for interventions to preserve it. In 1959, prompted by enquiries from members of the public and the Assynt District Council, the Ministry of Works recommended the offer of a small grant and the preparation of an architect's report, though the grant was not taken up at that time. It was not until the formation of a community group, Historic Assynt, which was made up of members of Assynt Community Council and Assynt Historical Society, that matters began to move forward. In 1997, under the aegis of Historic Assynt, the Inchnadamph Project was instigated. The project focused on Assynt's three important historic buildings: Ardvreck Castle itself; Calda House; and Inchnadamph Old Parish Church and the adjoining MacLeod Vault (the only remnant of the pre-1741 church). The church was to be restored as a centre for the interpretation of the buildings and of the social, cultural and religious history of the Loch Assynt area, while Ardvreck and Calda would be conserved and access provided to them. In 1997, the Forres office of Law and Dunbar-Nasmith Architects, led by Andrew Wright, was appointed to the project team to carry out a feasibility study.

Because of the scale of the project, funding was a significant issue. However, largely due to the efforts of Maggie Campbell of Historic Assynt, funding from the Heritage Lottery Fund was secured for project development, which allowed a project organiser to be appointed. Subsequently, in 2002, a grant of £409,000 was offered by the Heritage Lottery Fund towards the conservation of Ardvreck Castle and Calda House, and in order to provide public access to them. Historic Scotland was then able to offer a grant to the project, including £57,496 for the work on Ardvreck Castle itself. Funding for aspects of the project was also

Figure 8.2 Ardvreck Castle, an area of consolidated masonry

provided by Highland Council, Caithness and Sutherland Enterprise and a number of other Charitable Trusts. A significant amount of money was also raised locally by Historic Assynt.

In April 2003, the firm of Cumming and Co was appointed as contractor, and work began on site. As is almost invariably the case, stabilisation of the castle raised a number of challenges. The silhouette of the castle, with its distinctive turf-covered vaults and tall pinnacles of masonry, was an important part of the castle's aesthetic appeal. However, the unsupported sections of masonry were at risk of collapse, while the turf and rubble covering of the vaults was allowing water to percolate through the masonry, which was washing out the mortar. Once the castle had been scaffolded, the problems of the masonry became even more apparent (Fig 8.2), and it was found that the cement pointing had been obscuring cracks and collapsing joist pockets. As a consequence, the project required a higher level of engineering input than had been anticipated, and this was provided by John Addison, then of Peter Stephen and Partners.

Of particular concern in this respect were the upper storeys of the stair tower which was essentially a freestanding section of masonry with a significant outward lean. In order to stabilise the tower, the return of the adjacent wall on the east elevation was reconstructed and tied back into the original masonry to form a buttress, while a proprietary anchoring system was used to strengthen the wall itself. Another challenge was an area of overhanging masonry on the east elevation, which embodied evidence for a wall chamber. Rather than simply propping this, which would have been unsightly, a less intrusive metal bar supported by stainless steel wires was used to provide the necessary support.

Before deciding on the most appropriate way of water-proofing the broken vaults, several test pits were excavated by the project's archaeologist, Janet Hooper. As well as informing the methodology for water-proofing, this work demonstrated that the vaults were an insertion into the original tower. It was also found that the masses of rubble lying on the vault were firmly bonded, and it was consequently decided not to remove them, particularly since this would have altered the monument's appearance considerably. The approach adopted was to water-proof the masonry by repointing it before laying reinforced puddled clay on top of it, following which the original turf was relaid. The ground-floor chambers themselves were closed off with custom-made iron yetts, which would allow visitors to see into them, while limiting entry.

The work to Ardvreck Castle was completed in March 2005, and by September 2009 all of the original aims of the Inchnadamph project had been achieved. Both Ardvreck and Calda House have been consolidated and a new car park (with interpretation panels) to serve them has been formed, which blends in sensitively with the surrounding landscape. Inchnadamph Church has been restored and is now open to the public and is used for occasional services and weddings, while the adjacent MacLeod Vault has been conserved. Inevitably, in any project of this kind management and maintenance issues emerge that could not have been initially foreseen. At Ardvreck, the main problem has been erosion of the turf and puddled clay above the vaults, as a result of the greatly increased numbers of people climbing on them. Nevertheless, the project as a whole can be deemed to be a great success for the way that it has conserved the buildings, has encouraged more visitor access to the castle and associated sites, and has provided those visitors with a discreetly located car park and with information on the buildings and their history.

CHAPTER 9

Cessford Castle

Cessford, Roxburghshire, has one of the most formidable tower houses to have been erected in Scotland (Fig 1.5); indeed, in 1523 the leader of an English army deemed it to be the third strongest castle in Scotland (Fig 9.1). It is of L-shaped plan but is exceptionally complex in its layout. There was one entrance at ground-floor level in the east face of the main block, adjacent to the wing, and a second entrance at first-floor level in the north face of the wing. A stair ran the full height of the tower within the wall thickness at the re-entrant angle between the main block and wing, where it could be accessed from both entrances, and there was a second mural stair within the south wall, at the opposite junction of main block and wing. The main block housed a lofty barrel-vaulted hall, above a barrel-vaulted basement; there was a sequence of smaller chambers in the upper levels of the wing, above what appear to have been prison cells at the lowest levels, and a kitchen at first-floor level. There were mural closets at three of the corners of the hall, and ample provision of fireplaces throughout (Fig 9.2). Rather unusually for a Scottish tower house, a moulded base course was constructed around the foot of all but one of the external faces (Fig 9.3). The exception was the north face of the wing, which may suggest that provision was being made for a forebuilding of some kind in front of the entrances, which would perhaps have

Figure 9.1 Cessford Castle

been constructed in timber. Any evidence for that forebuilding was lost when walls were constructed at a later date to enclose the space in the angle between the main block and the wing.

The date of Cessford's tower is unknown. It is usually placed in the 15th century, and that may well be correct, since the first member of the Kerr of Altonburn family to style himself as 'of Cessford' did so in the mid-15th century. There are, however, a number of features that could point to an earlier date: these include the form of the hall fireplace and the foliage decoration of its caps, and also the provision of a base course. As has already been said, the latter is an unusual feature for a Scottish tower, and is most commonly found on a small number of relatively early towers, such as the oldest part of Clackmannan Tower (Clackmannanshire) or the fragmentary remains of the tower at Rowallan (Ayrshire). Perhaps even more importantly for a castle sited in the Borders, it is a feature found on a number of northern English towers of the mid- or later 14th century, including Chipchase and Langley. In considering the date, it should also be borne in mind that there must have been a residence at Cessford by the later 14th century, since there is an account of Sir Robert Ker being there when he heard of the death of Robert II in 1390. Nevertheless, the residence that he occupied at that time may not have been the present building, and we should therefore probably be prepared to keep an open mind about its date. At the top of the wing there is evidence of 16th-century reconstruction, with thin double walls corresponding to the thicker walls at the lower levels, the space between possibly serving as a wall-head firing gallery.

The tower stood at the centre of a more lightly walled enclosure of irregular plan, within which were several other buildings, together with a gatehouse referred to as a barbican in 1523. Sections of the courtyard wall still stand to the north of the tower, while elsewhere there are traces of banks where other

Figure 9.2 Cessford Castle, the interior, looking towards the hall fireplace

stretches of wall once stood, and also of a ditch. By the 16th century a major part of the outer strength of the castle must have been earthworks in front of the enclosure walls, which were known as 'vawmewres', and which would have been particularly effective in absorbing the cannon shot that was becoming a more significant factor in siege warfare in the early 16th century.

Located in the Borders, Cessford was within easy reach by English armies at periods of hostility between Scotland and its southern neighbour, and as a castle of the Warden of the Marches, Sir Andrew Kerr, it was an especially favoured target. The English are known to have taken the castle in 1519, 1523, 1543 and 1544, and it was presumably as a result of damage caused during one of those attacks that the superstructure of the tower house was partly rebuilt. But the main body of the tower appears to have escaped relatively unscathed, and the large fissures in the masonry that are now so evident are more likely to be the result of structural movement than of the impact of warfare (Fig 9.3).

In the course of the 20th century, the condition of the castle became a matter of some concern, and, as the costs of working on such buildings crept upwards, it became an increasing burden on its owner, the Duke of Roxburghe. In 1921 he offered it as a candidate for state guardianship; that was not possible at the time, though in 1936 it was scheduled as a monument of national importance. In 1954, when it seemed that works to stabilise the castle might be a possibility, a report by one of the Ministry of Works' architects was prepared, but the costs of £4000, which represented a considerable amount of money at the time, meant there was little prospect of this being taken forward. There were further discussions between the Ministry of Works and the owner in 1968, though again the increasingly high costs meant that nothing could be done.

Eventually, in 1999, when the tower's state was becoming a matter for real concern, on the advice of the Tweed Forum, Roxburghe Estates decided that something must be done to stabilise it in its existing condition. As a preliminary stage an advisory report was prepared by one of Historic Scotland's architects, which concluded that the total costs of everything that would be in the best interests of the castle could be upwards of £1,000,000. There was little likelihood of so much money being found, but it was decided that the best way forward would be to tackle those most urgent works that were placing the castle's long-term survival at risk, with the possibility of carrying out less urgent works in the future. A report on this basis was drawn up by the engineer John Addison, then of Peter Stephen and Partners, which was initially costed at £300,000, and a grant of 50% of this total was sought from Historic Scotland. Overall management of the project was placed in the hands of Luke Comins of the Tweed Forum, who was able to attract other substantial grants from the Heritage Lottery Fund, Objective Two European funding and the Landfill Tax, in addition to the funding provided by Roxburghe Estates, the owners.

As an initial stage, consent was granted for urgent works to be carried out at the wall head in April 2002, and it was agreed that the definitive project should start in 2004, with work extending over two years. In due course Krystyna Pytasz, of Peter Stephen and Partners (later of Waterman HDC, and now of

Figure 9.3 Cessford Castle, building breaks in the masonry

Addison Conservation and Design), was appointed project engineer, and the firm of Graeme Brown was awarded the masonry contract. Archaeological recording was to be carried out by Kirkdale Archaeology. Historic Scotland offered grants of £74,473 in 2004–05 and £69,281 in 2005–06, with a supplementary offer of £6000 in the second phase.

As has been said, the aim of the work was to stabilise the tower in its existing condition, involving as little stone replacement as possible, and, perverse as this might seem to those unfamiliar with work of this kind, the best outcome of such an intervention is that the building looks very much the same on completion of the work as it had done before work started. It was decided that nothing should be done where the existing state posed no problems. Thus, at the wall head all woody growths had to be removed to prevent further penetration of the wall core, and where there were signs of distress the naturally seeded turf topping was removed to permit consolidation of the underlying masonry, before being replaced and secured with netting. Where there was no evidence of distress, the turf topping was allowed to remain in place (see Fig 9.1). Inside the tower the work presented an enticing opportunity to carry out archaeological lowering of ground levels and overburdens, and doubtlessly much would have been learned about the castle in the process. Yet, since those raised ground levels and overburdens presented no threat to the building, to lower them would have required an open-ended and potentially costly archaeological project, followed by expensive additional consolidation, and it was decided that this could not be justified.

The greatest threat to the building's survival was recognised as a series of major fissures that had opened up, which had also destabilised the masonry associated with a number of voids in the walls, including window embrasures and mural closets. Initially it had been thought it would be necessary to insert considerable numbers of stainless steel tie rods across these fissures. In the event it proved possible to reduce the number of anchors, with much of the required stabilisation achieved through traditional masonry techniques. The new stonework required within the fissures was slightly set back from the wall face so that it was identifiable as such.

One initially unlooked-for bonus of scaffolding the whole building as a prelude to consolidating the masonry was the opportunity it gave to examine the fabric more closely than had previously been feasible. As a result, it became possible to build up a clearer picture of the likely sequence by which the various parts of the building may have been raised, on the evidence of changes in the character of the masonry and of breaks of coursing. Here it must be remembered that lime-bonded rubble walls have to be built up relatively slowly if the masonry is not to collapse before the mortar has dried, and not only might different sources of stone be used in successive phases, but the work might also have been carried out by different teams of masons. The resultant masonry changes are often very slight, but they may be visible on close inspection, though it should be remembered that when the building was complete such changes would have been hidden by the lime render with which masonry was almost invariably covered, and which is still partially in evidence at Cessford (see Fig 11.5). Nevertheless, the changes which are again in evidence once the lime render has been lost can be very telling.

As would be expected, in the first phase of operations the lowest walls of both the main block and the wing were evidently laid out together. Once the lower walls had been set out, however, the main effort appears to have been directed towards building up the wing rather than the main block, presumably so that the chambers in the wing could be occupied as soon as they were finished, and there is evidence in the masonry to suggest that two stages of the wing were built up before work resumed on the main block. Supplementing the evidence of the masonry changes, it seems that, as the wing was built up, seating was provided for the vault that it was intended to build over the basement below the hall; this seating took the form of a ledge in the wall on the west side of the wing, where the vault could eventually be based. This suggests there was no expectation that the rest of the vault would be built in the immediate future, since elsewhere when the lower walls of the hall basement were eventually built up to a sufficient height, the lower parts of the vault were bonded in with the walls in the way that would usually be expected. It was perhaps only when a fourth stage of the wing was reached that work resumed on the main block, and, for the first time, at this stage the masonry of the wing and the main block were continuously coursed through along the south wall. However, while the wing was to be carried still higher, it is unclear from what has survived if the main block was ever taken up beyond the handsomely proportioned hall on the first floor, which was covered by a second level of vaulting.

CHAPTER 10

Invergarry Castle

The ruin of Invergarry Castle in Inverness-shire, the residence of the McDonnells of Glengarry, stands on *Creagan an Fhithich*, the Rock of the Raven, on the shore of Loch Oich (Fig 1.6; Fig 10.1). (The family's motto, *Creagan an Fhithich*, together with their heraldic crest of a raven on a rock, thus evidently refers to the site of the castle.) In its present form the castle dates largely from after 1654, in which year the previous castle on the site was burnt by the parliamentary forces of General Monck. Rebuilding was probably carried out by the mason Robert Nicholson, possibly incorporating parts of what had survived of the previous castle.

In the later 17th and 18th centuries the chiefs of Glengarry were staunch Jacobites, as a result of which possession of the castle was forfeited on three separate occasions. In the 1690s the castle was garrisoned by government troops during one Jacobite uprising, following which in 1704 Glengarry petitioned unsuccessfully for the return of his home and compensation for damage done by the 'disorderly carriage of the souldiers'. Having eventually regained the castle, in 1716 it was again seized by government troops and was accidentally burned. In 1727, Thomas Rawlinson, an iron master of the Backbarrow Iron Co, who had established an iron furnace in the vicinity, repaired the structure as a residence for himself. However, in 1731 he agreed to return it to Glengarry, on the understanding that the latter would protect Rawlinson, his servants, tenants and employees from 'all thefts, incursions attempts or depradations'. In the aftermath of Culloden, in 1746, the castle was sacked and partially blown up by the Duke of Cumberland's troops, as part of the government's systematic 'pacification' of the Highlands. It was never reoccupied.

In 1838, the Glengarry portion of the McDonnell estates was sold to the Marquess of Huntly. In 1860 it was sold on, to Edward Ellice, who built a new house nearby in 1866–69 to the designs of David Bryce, and this is now the Glengarry Castle Hotel. The castle itself was to remain in the possession of the Glengarry Mcdonells until 1991 when it was acquired by the MacCallum family, the owners of the hotel.

The castle was surveyed by Lewis Petit for the Board of Ordnance in 1741, when it was still roofed, and his plan and elevation give the best impression of its appearance when complete (Fig 10.2). It is set out to a stepped L-plan, and was of five storeys with a sixth at the north-east corner. It is constructed of gneiss boulders with red sandstone dressings and quoins, and there are considerable traces of harling. The main entrance was on the east side of the north-west wing, where an imposing great stair that was built around an open well led to the large first-floor hall in the main block. Petit's plan seems to show an aisle or gallery

Figure 10.1 Invergarry Castle (John Malcolm)

of some form running along the entrance side of the hall. The upper floors were reached by a scale-and-platt stair in the re-entrant angle of the main block and the north-west wing, and also by a circular stair tower at the south-east corner. Above a later stair in the north-west wing there would have been further chambers. The arrangement of the stairs would have allowed a high degree of privacy of access to all of the upper chambers.

As would be expected by the mid-17th century, the castle did not have a parapet, but the wall head was elaborated by turreted studies at the some of the angles. The circular stair was also taken up into an extra storey and this additional floor was corbelled out to the square, having gables finished with crow steps. The plan, together with features such as the imposing staircase and the turret studies, displays some similarities with Castle Leslie (Aberdeenshire) and Innes House (Moray), both of the mid-17th century.

By the later 19th century the abandoned castle was becoming increasingly ruinous; indeed, its south-east corner, a portion of the west wing and much of the upper storey had collapsed before 1889. Early attempts at stabilisation of the fabric involved the insertion of iron straps at the top of the stair tower, and some of the stairs were capped with concrete. These works may have been undertaken at the behest of the Ellice family. In 1989 a report on its structural condition was commissioned by the Invergarry Trust from the engineers Gavin Walker and Associates. This confirmed the castle's fragile state, and offered an approach to safeguarding its future, Unfortunately, this came too late to save the stair tower, which collapsed in 1995. By that time the castle was owned by the MacCallum family, which was anxious to preserve the castle for the future.

Conservation work, supported by grant assistance from Historic Scotland, was eventually initiated in March 2005, under the direction of Krystyna Pytasz, then of Waterman HDC, in the course of which a number of innovative techniques were employed. The first phase consisted of emergency works targeting the most fragile areas of the stair tower. Self-compacting sand was used to shore up its surviving ground-floor vault, and was pumped into voids in the tumble to help support the massive loads of collapsed masonry. Temporary props and lime-filled bags were used to hold up the east side of the vault and to support the inner skin of the north wall, which was extremely fragile because of the loss of the surrounding masonry and lintel of the fireplace.

Once the main campaign of works was instigated, the principal block of the castle was deemed to be particularly vulnerable, since it had lost much of the

Figure 10.2 Invergarry Castle, the Board of Ordnance survey, 1741 (courtesy of the Trustees of the National Library of Scotland)

RENEWED LIFE FOR SCOTTISH CASTLES

Figure 10.3 Invergarry Castle, the beams inserted to stabilise the fabric (Krystyna Pytasz)

Figure 10.4 Invergarry Castle, a relieving arch made up of lime bags

structural support once provided by a combination of its south-east corner, the west wing and the stair tower. In order to brace the masonry, six composite stainless steel and hardwood beams were installed into existing joist pockets at the second- and third-floor levels, with the purpose of tying the two sides of the structure together (Fig 10.3). Two large cranes had to be deployed for this purpose. Stainless steel anchors were also drilled into the sand-filled vault below the stair to support this area.

Much work was directed to consolidating the three surviving walls of the main block, largely using more traditional techniques, and involving a great deal of repointing with lime mortar and reinsertion of lost pinnings. However, there were a number of areas where other techniques had to be used because of the extreme fragility of the masonry. There were two areas of particular concern: the chimney breast above the hall fireplace, which had already been propped, and an area around a window opening in the circular stair tower. In these areas the masonry had lost much of its lime mortar and pinnings, and because of their rounded profile many of the stones had become extremely loose. As a consequence, rebuilding in traditional lime-pointed masonry proved to be impossible, and instead hessian bags filled with a lime concrete mixture of aggregate with a lime binder were used (Fig 10.4). In an unset state these bags have the advantage that they readily mould themselves to the surviving masonry, but they can be inserted with less risk of creating further instability. When set they provide the necessary support, and the hessian can then be removed and the lime concrete dressed back. As an intervention it is an obviously modern repair, but is sympathetic both in terms of the softness of material in relation to the original masonry, and of its appearance. This method was only used where traditional techniques would have carried a clear risk of further destabilising the masonry.

The wall heads and other exposed surfaces were capped with puddled clay and turf, an approach that, as has already been said, is increasingly seen as having wide applications in conservation projects. At high levels nylon netting was pinned into masonry joints in order to reduce the risk of future masonry falls from areas unlikely to be subject to regular inspection.

The total cost of the project was about £180,800, of which Historic Scotland contributed £132,642. As a result of the work that has been carried out, a castle that had been on the very brink of major collapse has been successfully stabilised. In carrying out this work, the MacCallum family has not only sought to preserve a romantically beautiful and historically highly significant ruin, but has also aimed to provide safe public access and an appropriate level of visitor information. As a further part of this, the family hopes to build a timber viewing platform in the south-east corner of the castle to allow visitors to see the interior of the castle safely without having to climb over the areas of consolidated tumble.

Section Three
Restoring Castles

CHAPTER II

Introductory comments

A number of the questions that almost invariably have to be asked in the early stages of restoring castles have already been touched upon in the previous section, and particularly in the introductory comments to that section in Chapter 4. This third section of the book will now consider a number of projects in which castles have been restored for a variety of new roles, and where the work has consequently gone beyond simple conservation. Amongst the roles that were the end result of the process of restoration, Aikwood (Selkirkshire), Balgonie (Fife), Kisimul (Barra), Melgund (Angus) and Towie Barclay (Aberdeenshire) became private family homes (see Figs 18.1–18.2; 16.1–16.3; 12.1–12.3; 20.1–20.4; 14.1–14.5); Hallbar (Lanarkshire) and Liberton (Midlothian) have been adapted as holiday accommodation (see Figs 21.1–21.3; 19.1–19.2); Rossend (Fife) serves as an office (see Figs 17.1–17.5); Castle Menzies (Perthshire) is a clan centre that is available for a range of uses (see Figs 15.1–15.3); Monimail (Fife) is put to community use (see Figs 22.1–22.2); and the great hall at Stirling Castle is at the heart of one of Scotland's most significant historic visitor attractions (see Figs 13.1–13.6).

In the case of Kisimul, Balgonie and Melgund, the castles were roofless ruins at the time work was started, and indeed some of the buildings at the last two remain in a ruined state today. In general, however, the most straightforward restoration projects are at buildings that are structurally relatively complete, or that are not so far ruined as to make it difficult to establish any of their historical architectural forms. Indeed, at both Castle Menzies and Rossend the buildings had still been occupied as family homes until relatively recently, though at Rossend the castle was coming close to being so derelict by the time of its restoration that the prospects for its continued existence were looking highly doubtful. In the altogether exceptional case of the great hall in the castle of Stirling, it had remained in use as a military barrack into the 1960s, though that use had so extensively distorted its original architectural character that extensive research was required to establish if it could be restored to its overwhelmingly important primary state. In several cases the buildings had survived through being put to agricultural uses of various kinds, as at Aikwood, Liberton, Towie Barclay and to a lesser extent at Monimail. Such mundane uses can in fact be more benign than might be thought, since they usually mean that, while a certain level of regular basic maintenance has had to be carried out, there has been little likelihood of major structural interventions, other than the cutting of a number of new openings, as may be seen at Aikwood. By contrast, at Hallbar, there was a major and somewhat over-creative restoration in the mid-19th century, which left the historic authenticity of some of its details in doubt.

An essential starting point for any proposal for restoration is to assemble as much information on the building and its context as possible, so that all decisions are informed by a high level of understanding. This may well require engaging the services of a number of specialists who are experienced in work of this kind. Historians, together with architectural historians or archaeologists, are likely to be needed to trawl through the documentation associated with the site and to undertake a first analysis of the surviving architectural evidence. At the same time that the preliminary research is initiated, it is generally a good idea for an architect or surveyor to make a start on the detailed survey of the building that will form the basis for all further considerations. This will involve the preparation of plans, elevations, cross-sections, profiles of moulded details, and full photographic coverage. Particular attention needs to be paid to areas that are potentially of great significance for the understanding of the building, such as the evidence for floors, partitions, the form of the fenestration, and wall finishes. Evidence is also likely to be encountered of the ways in which the building has been modified in the course of its history, and in this the services of a structural archaeologist or architectural historian will certainly be of great benefit. It is unlikely that any first survey can be comprehensive, however, since access to the upper levels and wall heads may only be achievable once work has started, while subsequent archaeological excavation of ground levels and overburdens may expose evidence at initially concealed lower levels.

There may also be a need for some preliminary investigative archaeological excavation. In general archaeological work is best postponed until it is reasonably certain that restoration will take place, since, however carefully it is planned and carried out, all archaeology is inherently destructive. However, preliminary investigations may be an unavoidable means of establishing the planning of missing elements that will eventually have to be reinstated. In due course full excavation will be required of all areas and overburdens that may have to be disturbed as part of the restoration and the provision of services. Beyond that, if there are to be new buildings in the vicinity of the restored castle, it is generally best if they reflect the planning, scale and massing of buildings that had been there previously, so it is important to investigate the evidence for those buildings. There may also eventually be a case for archaeological investigation of the wider context if there is any likelihood of reinstating the historic arrangement of courtyards and gardens that were usually associated with a castle. Nevertheless, on grounds of both conservation and cost, it may be best to limit excavation to no more than what is required for properly informed restoration to take place.

Once all the initial information has been put together, possibly in the form of the first part of a conservation plan, it is necessary to give careful consideration to the range of options that would meet the castle's structural needs, before deciding if restoration is indeed in its best interests. If it is concluded that restoration *will* meet the castle's long-term needs most appropriately, the next stage is for an architect or surveyor who is experienced in such work to develop detailed proposals, in close consultation with the bodies that have a statutory concern. In working up those proposals, so far as possible everything should be based on the evidence found within the castle itself, and that has been recorded on the survey. But it may also be helpful to look to other castles of similar date and scale, and in the same geographical area, if those castles can provide supplementary comparative evidence.

Of the masonry elements of a castle, the most vulnerable parts are generally at the wall head, and one of the most common losses is of the parapet that ran around the outer edge of any wall walk there may have been. Parapets always had to be more slightly constructed than the rest of the walls, so that as much space as possible could be allowed for the wall walks behind them. Some earlier parapets appear to have taken the form of a simple vertical continuation of the line of the lower walls, as seems to have been the case at Liberton (see Fig 19.1). By the 15th century, however, it had become more usual to project them outwards on a corbel table, which might be given considerable decorative embellishment. Indeed, as greater architectural emphasis was given to the upper silhouette of castles in the course of the 15th and 16th centuries, the parapet was perhaps the feature that was most likely be modified in response to changing fashions, though one of the consequences of this is that restoring a parapet to an incorrect form or with inappropriate materials can create a particularly misleadingly image of a castle.

So far as the castles discussed below are concerned, at Balgonie the crenellated parapet had been lost relatively recently, which meant that there were both photographs and drawings that showed it when complete, and it could be restored with a high degree of accuracy (see Fig 16.1). Conversely, at Liberton nothing was known of how the parapet had been finished, and it was decided that the least misleading course was to restore it as a wall that was finished and coped on a horizontal line (see Fig 19.1). Additional justification for that approach can be found in the fact that, since the merlons were the most vulnerable part of a crenellated parapet, it was not uncommon for them to be lost or removed, so that the restoration of the parapet as a simple wall is not necessarily historically inappropriate. However, at some particularly highly finished castles the parapet must always have been such an important part of the total appearance that to restore the castle without its wall-head crenellations would greatly detract from the final appearance. At Melgund there was the added factor that balusters were found in the course of restoration, and this raised the possibility that at one stage there had been a balustrade at the wall head. On balance, any such balustrade was deemed unlikely to have dated from the main building campaign, and a crenellated parapet was reinstated, with its details based on those to be found at other high-status castles of the mid-16th century (see Fig 20.1).

Moving on to consider less permanent parts of the building, although timber floors have almost invariaby been lost in any roofless ruin, their structure is generally at least partly represented in the surviving masonry, though caution is required in interpreting the evidence. If it can be seen, for example, that the floors were supported by corbels, it might be assumed that those corbels carried the joists directly, and if there are pockets in the walls immediately above the corbels, that probably was indeed the case. Yet even in such a seemingly straightforward case, the situation might be more complex than first appears. Thus, if the corbels are quite widely spaced, it may be that there were principal joists running in one direction, with secondary joists above and at right angles to them. The situation might be even more complex than that, because the corbels may have supported a wall plate, which in turn supported the joists. In such cases it may be possible to identify additional evidence in the location of the corbels in relation to any doorway thresholds above them, which might indicate if there is enough depth for both a wall plate and a joist, or for no more than a joist. Comparative evidence from related sites can be of great help in such cases, though it should be remembered that floor construction often varied from one level to another even in a single building, and evidence found at one level may be no indication of what happened at other levels.

Timber was more widely used in castles than is often assumed. It is sometimes forgotten, for example, that the upper floors of many larger tower houses were more subdivided than the lower floors, with that subdivision generally achieved by timber and plaster partitions that were light enough to be supported by the floor joists. Amongst other timber features, there may also have been screens at the service end of the hall or draught enclosures around the doorways of chambers. Occasionally a ghost of these is left in surviving plasterwork, or the metal fixings by which they were attached to the walls may be still embedded in the masonry. All too often, however, there are no more indicators of the erstwhile existence of a partition than the fact that an upper room has two fireplaces, or that there are two latrine closets, particularly if they are set closely together so that they could share the same waste chute. It is important to understand such evidence for the historic internal planning, because it is generally more satisfactory for the layout of a restored castle to follow the arrangements that existed when it was built or last occupied if the proportions of the rooms are to work best. In some cases, it may prove necessary to introduce partitions for which there is no historic authority if the building is to meet modern requirements for privacy and safety. At Hallbar, for example, a corridor had to be created to provide access from one stair to another.

The timber feature that tends to survive least well is the roof, since it was the part that was most exposed to the elements. At one of the castles considered in this section, Aikwood, the roof had survived relatively intact, and there it was possible to repair and retain it, with only minor adjustments to some of the collars in one area (Fig 11.1). On the whole, Scottish domestic roof design was not particularly complex, and the majority of roofs seem to have had a regular succession of identical rafters, each with a simple triangle formed by sole-pieces and ashlar posts or wall posts at the base of the rafters, combined with one or two levels of collars at the upper levels. In roofs of this kind there was seldom any greater longitudinal bracing than the sarking boards. However, over the great hall at Stirling Castle there was one of the most complex roofs ever built in late medieval Scotland, in which the principal rafters were of hammer-beam construction. This roof had been destroyed when the hall was adapted as a barrack in about 1800, though 18th-century survey drawings recorded the appearance of its principal rafters (see Fig 13.3), which showed it to have had many similarities with the contemporary roof over the great hall of Edinburgh Castle (see Fig 3.8). On the basis of the drawings and the comparative evidence it was therefore possible to restore it with a high level of historic accuracy (see Fig 13.6).

One of the other partly timber features that can cause difficulty in castle restoration projects is the fenestration. In the principal rooms of most later medieval castles and tower houses the upper two-thirds of the window opening was glazed, with small rectangular or lozenge-shaped panes held together by lead kames that were set directly into chases in the stonework of the window openings and braced by saddle bars. On the inner side within the embrasures of windows of this kind there was usually a frame set into a rebate, within which was hung one or two levels of shutters, the lower level corresponding to the void below the glazing, and the upper level – if there was one – closing against the glazing. The problem of such fenestration is that the closest attention to detailing is required to make it draught- and rain-proof, while for modern tastes there can be the disadvantage that it permits only a limited amount of light through window openings that are already generally quite small. In later castles windows tended to become considerably larger, while at earlier castles the main windows were often enlarged to permit more light, and such windows are generally closer to modern preferences. It might be added that later forms of glazing became progressively more efficient and, after a period when hinged casements were the favoured choice, sliding sash-and-case windows began to be fitted from around the turn of the 17th and 18th centuries. Thus, at Castle Menzies, Monimail and Rossend, sash windows had already been installed before restoration began, and there was no reason to consider replacing them by anything different.

In those cases where a tower that is to be restored has retained evidence for nothing other than fixed glazing and shutters, it is generally best to reinstate fenestration of that kind, and this has been done at both Liberton and Melgund.

Figure 11.1 Aikwood Tower, the roof as seen within the attic bedroom

In other cases a level of compromise has been adopted. It is frequently found, for example, that the chases into which the glazing was set are now too decayed to be able to receive the glazing safely, and one solution in such cases has been to set the glazing into a shutter frame that is deeper than would be required for the shutters alone. So far as dealing with the low levels of lighting permitted through such fenestration is concerned, one possible means of gaining additional light is to have glazed panels in the lower shutters, as appears to have been done from the start in some continental examples. This does mean, however, that in the interests of privacy it may be preferable to have a smaller shutter set within the body of the main shutter at the lower level, as has been done in parts of Melgund (Fig 11.2).

Figure 11.2 Melgund Castle, a restored shuttered window

One of the recurring issues that tends to arise in the course of castle restoration projects is that of finding ways to make sufficiently clear what is historic and what is modern insertion or replacement. Although it might be argued that new work will retain a pristine appearance for a long period, and will therefore continue to bespeak its newness, in due course it will almost invariably lose that lack of patina and thus become less easily distinguishable from the historic fabric. Taking account of this, and in view of the fact that a building has to be regarded in some senses as a document that can tell us much about the periods at which it was built and about how it was intended to be used, it is particularly important that as little as possible is done that might disturb or confuse the evidence it embodies. While it probably has to be accepted that it is almost inevitable there should be some level of disturbance of evidence in the course of a restoration project, that makes it especially important to take all possible measures to ensure that what is modern disturbance or intrusion can be identified as such.

To some extent this can be achieved by keeping the fullest possible records of whatever is done, and by depositing those records in publicly accessible archives. Nevertheless, no matter how carefully they are curated, records can be – and sometimes are – lost or damaged in the course of time, and so every effort should be made to incorporate evidence for what has been done within the building itself. In doing so, a balance has to be struck between making that evidence sufficiently visible for those who might wish to seek it out, while not disfiguring the building in the process of making it visible. Amongst the ways in which this can be achieved, replacement features can have the date of their insertion discreetly inscribed at some point. Similarly, new areas of masonry can be differentiated by being outlined in tiles or slates set into the mortar around their perimeter, as was done in reinstating the parapet at Liberton. It may even be appropriate to set back the face of the new areas by a short distance, as was done at Cessford, while having the date inscribed on one of the stones within the new masonry.

One course that has occasionally been adopted is to use modern materials in locations where they would not be normally visible, but where the modern work would become identifiable if the castle became derelict at a later date. There have been cases, for example, of the use of concrete blocks instead of stone where it is to be harled externally or plastered internally. However, this is seldom satisfactory in external locations, since the regularity and unhistoric scale of the blocks is generally evident beneath the lime harling, especially when it is wet and the joints become more visible.

The decision on how to reinstate the lost wall-head parapet at Melgund provides a reminder of another problem inherent in castle restoration, and that is the decision that must often be taken as to which stage of a castle's history should be selected as the point that is to be represented. All of the evidence seems to suggest that Melgund was a single-period building, and yet the survival of a baluster could be taken to suggest that there had been some alterations at a later date. At Melgund there was insufficient evidence to be able to identify any such later stage with anything approaching certainty; but at a high proportion of castles there is clear evidence that they were modified in varying degrees and on more than one occasion. As a general rule, all significant stages of a castle's history deserve respect and should be retained in place, since they are as much a part of its history as the original building. But how do we decide what is significant and worthy of retention? At the great hall in Stirling Castle, its adaptation as a barrack in about 1800 casts a fascinating light on how a late medieval building might be adapted to meet the military needs of a much later generation (Fig 11.3). It might be argued that, since the hall was probably used for a longer period as a barrack than as the setting for great occasions of state in the 16th century, that later phase of its history should have been given precedence. And yet that adaptation was very widely regarded as having resulted in such massive disfigurement of an outstandingly important building that few were prepared to suggest it should be retained. Despite that, the decision to restore it to its primary state was only taken after the most careful analysis and research had established that this could be done with a high degree of authenticity, and in the course of the restoration all new work was carefully identified as such.

Most cases are less clear-cut than that of Stirling's great hall, even if they are usually less complex. At Castle Menzies, the 18th-century ranges to the rear of the main block were in such poor repair by the time the process of restoration was instigated that it would have been technically very difficult and extremely expensive to retain them. In the conservation climate of the time, when so many

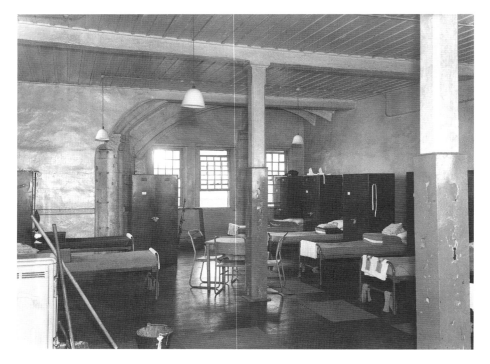

great country houses had already been – and were still being – lost, and when saving anything at Menzies was going to require such a major effort, it was decided in 1976 that there was no alternative to demolishing the greater part of those ranges. The large 19th-century wing to the west of the castle was also approaching a similar state of decay by that time, and for some years it looked as if there was little alternative to demolishing that part as well. Yet, as the conservation climate began to take on a more optimistic aspect in the 1980s, and as it came to be realised how significant this wing was for what it could tell about the early career of an important architect, it was decided that the effort should be made to retain it (see Fig 15.3). It could perhaps be argued that there has been a lack of consistency in demolishing one relatively late part of a house whilst keeping another, and it is certainly preferable if a completely consistent course can be followed. But, when what has been achieved at Menzies is seen, few would feel that the compromise has greatly devalued the end result, and in some ways it is of added interest for what it tells us about the developing conservation climate in the later 20th century.

There is a particular problem in deciding what should be kept of alterations that were made when a castle was reduced to serving a rather more menial function than was originally intended for it. While those modifications must certainly be regarded as a part of the building's history, as with the adaptation of the great hall at Stirling in *c* 1800, the consequences are often on balance deemed to have been largely negative. Even so, the value of those modifications should not be dismissed without the most careful consideration. At Aikwood, for example, the later works had involved the addition of a farmhouse that was subsequently converted to a byre, and also the cutting of a number of new openings in the tower house (Fig 11.4). Since the byre was to be retained for the additional space it could provide, it also made sense to retain the later openings in the tower house itself. This was both in the interests of enhanced consistency in the phase that was to be represented, and more practically because this made the tower house basement altogether more easily usable.

The materials employed in building a castle were usually limited to a relatively narrow pallette of locally available stone, lime and timber, and this should be reflected in the choice of materials employed in the process of restoration wherever possible. The external finishes played a particularly visible part in the appearance the castle presented. The masonry of Scottish castles was probably invariably rendered over with a lime coating that is usually referred to as harling, and this was usually of a very similar composition to the mortar that was used for bonding the masonry. A porous coating of this kind made the walls more resistant to the retention of rainwater while allowing them to breathe, and aesthetically it gave a visual homogeneity to the building as a whole. Harling was almost invariably finished with a thinner lime-wash, which would have been renewed at more or less regular intervals. At Cessford, there is clear evidence that the harling must have extended over both the rubble masonry of the walls and the dressed stonework of features such as doorways and windows (Fig 11.5), though it was perhaps more thinly applied over those features so that any carved or moulded detail remained visible.

Figure 11.4 Aikwood Tower and the byre range

By the 19th century, however, many owners of castles preferred the appearance of exposed masonry, and harling was often systematically removed as a result. This evidently happened at Castle Menzies, though the removal of additions to the rear of the castle in 1976 exposed fascinating evidence for the harling that had once covered both the rubble-built walls and the ashlar corbelling that supported one of the turrets on that side of the castle. The case for reharling tends to attract vociferous support, since it is seen as an essential part of the character of many Scottish buildings. At Menzies, however, there were sound arguments for not reinstating the harling in the course of restoration, since there appears to have been a conscious decision to remove it at an important stage of its history. It was thus the later stages of the castle's architectural history that continued

Figure 11.5 Cessford Castle, the traces of harling

to be represented, but it would in any case have been historically inconsistent to adopt any other approach when the west wing of 1845–52, which had never been harled, was to be retained.

There can be other reasons for not reinstating harling. At Melgund, for example, where part of the building was restored and part conserved as a consolidated ruin, it would have been visually disruptive to reharl the restored parts but not the ruined parts, and the decision was taken to leave the stone exposed throughout (see Fig 20.1). A decision not to reharl was also taken for a number of reasons at Aikwood, Balgonie, Hallbar and Kisimul, though there is always the option of reharling them at a later date. It might in fact be argued that harling should only be reinstated if there is good evidence for its historic character, since to reinstate a visually prominent feature without that evidence would distort the understanding of the historic appearance of the building. Against that is the argument that harling protects and consolidates friable stone that will otherwise continue to decay.

In earlier attempts at reharling, as at Rossend and Towie Barclay, the importance of establishing the precise character of the materials was not yet appreciated, and standard types of finish were adopted; nor at that time was it appreciated that an important part of the role that harling had to play was its porosity. Consequently, new renders were often cement-based and thus impervious, and this has sometimes led to problems of water retention between the masonry and the harling. In more recent operations at Liberton, Monimail and the great hall at Stirling Castle, great efforts have been made to establish the composition of the harling through careful analysis of surviving fragmentary residues. The results that have been achieved permit an appearance for those buildings to be re-established that more closely approaches their historic state than anything that had previously been achieved. Even in those cases, however, the representation of a historic state can be no more than partial, since it is likely that certain details would once have been picked out in colour, including the parapet carvings at Monimail and the carved tabernacle heads at Stirling. Yet where there can be no certainty about additional colouring, it is almost invariably best to avoid speculative reinstatement, and if there is a wish to explain what may have been lost, this is probably best done by providing reconstruction sketches as part of an interpretative display.

A further factor that all castle owners have to confront, and that therefore should perhaps be at least touched on because of the impact it has had on a number of cases covered here, is that of personal safety. When the castles that are to be discussed below were built, this was an aspect that was probably given relatively little consideration, and it is therefore hardly surprising that it can be difficult to make such buildings conform to the current safety requirements of building regulations. Tower houses in which one room is stacked above another, and that are interconnected by nothing more than dark and narrow spiral stairs, as at Aikwood, or steep mural stairs with irregular steps, as at Hallbar, can be virtually impossible to negotiate for anyone with mobility problems. It is only at castles such as Menzies and Rossend, where more of the principal accommodation extends laterally at first-floor level, and there is a spacious stair up to that level, that the problem is less acute. Current legislation requires reasonable measures to be taken to permit disabled access, but this would generally not require changes that might significantly modify the historic character of the building. At Rossend, where relatively large numbers of people are employed within a busy architects' office, and there is thus an unavoidable need to meet fire regulations, provision for emergency evacuation was met by a modern tubular stair projecting at the far end of the building from the main stair (see Fig 17.1). At the diminutive tower of Hallbar, however, where holiday use was the end in view, there was no realistic scope for either disabled access or a secondary emergency stair. The solution adopted was to provide accommodation for the less agile in an adjacent building with ground-floor access, and to create a garret above a fire-proof vault as a refuge within the tower itself in case of fire.

Having taken an overview of some of the factors that had to be taken into account in restoring the castles considered in this book, we shall move on to consider what has been done at those castles individually.

CHAPTER 12

Kisimul Castle

Kisimul Castle occupies a site that is extraordinarily attractive to modern eyes: a small rock islet in Castle Bay, about 200m off the southern shore of the Hebridean island of Barra (Fig 1.7; Fig 12.1). It was the seat of the Macneils of Barra, who held their lands under the Lords of the Isles. The castle takes the form of an enclosure defined by a high curtain wall, the irregular plan of which was governed by the configuration of the islet. In its final form there were ranges of buildings around almost the entire extent of the inner face of the curtain wall, though the only feature to rise significantly above the wall is a rectangular tower house. On the western mainland of Scotland, castles in which a high curtain wall grows almost organically out of a rock outcrop in this way have a history going back to at least the 13th century, and a number of commentators have suggested such an early date for Kisimul. However, the basic form of the castle should perhaps be seen as having been adopted largely as a response to the restrictions imposed by the site itself, rather than as an indication of a regionalised approach to castle design at any one period. On balance, and taking account of the known history of the site and of the few diagnostically significant architectural details, it seems most likely that it was built after Barra was granted to Gill-Adhamnain Macneill by Alexander Macdonald, Lord of the Isles, in 1427.

The castle was built throughout of locally quarried rubble, bonded with lime mortar, which would initially have been rendered over and lime-washed. On the evidence of the relationship between the tower house and the curtain wall, the earliest of the buildings on the site was almost certainly the former (Fig 12.2). It stands at the south-east angle of the enclosure and rises through three storeys above a battered plinth. The tower's basement is separately entered from the courtyard, and any communication with the upper floors can only have been by means of a trap door. It is not clear how access to the first-floor main entrance was achieved when the tower was first built, but eventually it was rather awkwardly contrived by a forestair against its north wall that led to the adjacent curtain wall, and from there it seems a timber stair must have risen to the entrance. Access to the second floor and wall head was by means of a mural stair that rose in two short flights at the north-west angle of the tower. The upper floors were provided with latrines but no fireplaces, and it is assumed that the chambers would have been heated by braziers. The crenellated wall head of the tower was evidently rebuilt in the later Middle Ages, incorporating a box machicolation in the north wall, above the entrance.

The curtain wall was probably first built around the central decades of the 15th century, not long after the tower, but the evidence has been confused

Figure 12.1 Kisimul Castle (© Crown copyright)

Figure 12.2 Kisimul Castle, the courtyard

by the extent to which it was rebuilt in the mid-20th century at its western end. The original entrance to the courtyard through the curtain wall was in a short stretch of wall immediately adjacent to the north-east angle of the tower house. Along the wall head at a number of points there is evidence for the seating of timber galleries, evidence that rarely survives and is therefore of great interest. Some of the ranges abutting the curtain wall may have been approximately contemporary with the wall, including a two-storeyed building on the north-west side of the courtyard that is now referred to as a hall, and a narrower range on the north-east side that has been restored as a chapel. Adjoining the west side of the tower is a later two-storeyed range that may have incorporated a kitchen. The extent of modern restoration has made it difficult to form a clear idea of the likely date of the other ranges within the castle, though it is probable that some of the work is as late as the 16th and 17th centuries. At the south-west corner is the rebuilt range that has come to be known as the Tanist's (heir's) House, while to the north-east of the tower are the remains of what is generally referred to as the Gokman's (watchman's) House, though neither of those identifications appears to have any firm historical basis. On the east side of the castle, outside the curtain wall, are traces of a boat haven and what may have been a boathouse.

Figure 12.3 Kisimul Castle, before restoration (© RCAHMS. SC 1205611, Licensor www.rcahms.gov.uk)

The castle remained sufficiently defensible into the late 17th century for unwelcome government officials to be denied access in 1675, and, according to an account of his personal experience during a visit by Martin Martin twenty years later, strangers were still being discouraged from entering. By the middle of the 18th century, however, the castle was no longer either habitable or defensible, and its floors and roofs were finally to be destroyed by a fire in 1795. The progress of its subsequent ruination was accelerated by the way in which its masonry was robbed to provide ballast for the fleet of fishing boats that operated from Barra (Fig 12.3). It was only after the castle was acquired by Robert Macneil, an American architect, whose claim to be the Macneil of Barra had been formally recognised by the Lord Lyon in 1915, that the process was first halted and then reversed.

Kisimul was scheduled in 1934, when it was in the ownership of Lady Cathcart, whose father-in-law, Colonel Gordon of Cluny, had acquired the estate in 1838. Macneil had already been endeavouring to purchase it for some years, with a view to restoring it as a clan headquarters and occasional residence, and he was eventually successful in this in 1937, following Lady Cathcart's death. In the following year he directed his unbounded enthusiasm into clearing out the courtyard and making a start on consolidating the most precarious masonry. The Inspector and Architect of the Ministry of Works expressed some concern about the damage that might be caused in both aspects of this, especially as the excavation was taking place without archaeological supervision, and the consolidation was being carried out using a high level of cement. The new owner was persuaded by the Ministry that he should submit proposals for what he was planning to do, and in 1939 the eminent architect Reginald Fairlie was asked to report on those proposals. However, the outbreak of war prevented further work being carried out for some years, though by then the not inconsiderable sum of £3000 had already been spent.

Work eventually resumed in earnest in 1954, and grant assistance was successfully sought from the Historic Buildings Council. The estimated costs were £5000 for the so-called Tanist's House at the south-west corner, of which only fragments survived, but which was to be restored as a first residence for the owner, and £2000 for filling in a major breach in the curtain wall. Work began on the wall in 1956, and on the house in 1957, with the latter being structurally complete the following year. The owner's attention then moved on to the adjoining range, along the north-west side of the enclosure. Although this had clearly been a two-storeyed building, it was decided to treat it as a hall; by the end of 1958 structural work was well advanced, but it was only completed in 1959, when suitable slates were eventually procured for the roof.

The tower house was to be the most contentious part of the work. In 1959 the Ministry of Works' architect said that the necessary work to stabilise the tower was likely to cost around £2500, and in 1962 both the Ancient Monuments Board and Historic Buildings Council recommended that the operation should be limited to consolidation of the surviving fabric rather than full restoration. It was also suggested that the work should be carried out by the Ministry's own workmen, who had great experience in such operations, though it was made clear that pressures of work would mean this could not be done for some time. However, by 1966, it still had not been possible to allocate a team of masons to the project, and, since Macneil had been able to obtain some funding for the work, he was anxious to move ahead. By 1967, although the Ancient Monuments Board considered his proposals for dealing with the tower inadequate, he decided to reinstate the floors and roof. At the same time restoration was being carried out to other buildings around the courtyard, including the building that it was decided to treat as a chapel on the north-east side. The main bulk of work was completed by 1970.

The restoration of Kisimul was the work of a highly energetic and deeply committed single-minded individual, who took a very serious view of his role as Chief of Clan Neil. He worked against extraordinary difficulties that resulted from the remoteness and inaccessibility of the site, from the difficulty of procuring adequate funding at a time of escalating costs, and from the fact that he was able to spend only a small amount of time on Barra in each year that he visited. It is perhaps also the case that a castle such as Kisimul, which is completely surrounded by the sea, and is in an area that is not notable for its clement weather, can never have been easy to live in, and it certainly did not readily lend itself to modern ideas of comfort. Nevertheless, a number of aspects of the work caused continuing disquiet. The restored crenellation was regarded by many as misrepresenting the castle's historic state, as were the way in which the building identified as a chapel was restored with a timber superstructure, and the north-east range was restored as a single-storey hall. There was also some concern at the widespread use of concrete, though this was perhaps understandable on a site where there was little prospect of preventing water penetration altogether.

From the delightful book that he wrote when restoration of Kisimul was well advanced, *Castle in the sea*, it is clear that Macneil had his own very firm views on the history of his castle. He was deeply unhappy with the analysis published in the *Inventory* of the Royal Commission on the Ancient and Historical Monuments of Scotland, regretting that 'so many errors regarding the castle occur in the description'. This was largely because the Commission had dated the castle later than Macneil believed could be justified; it was his view that the curtain wall had originated in the 11th century, and the tower in the 12th. Nevertheless, even though Macneil was well aware that not everyone agreed with his approach, he was invariably generous in his response, and even invited one of his critical friends, Sir Iain Moncreiffe of that Ilk, to write the foreword to his book.

It is beyond question that his approach to restoration was in no sense drily academic, and he said that one of his guiding principles was 'to consider what modernisation would have taken place if my family had continued to live in the castle after 1748'. It is additionally important to remember that he approached the work as a practising architect who was aware of the structural problems likely to stem from the use of materials requiring regular maintenance, and it must always be recognised that his contributions to the castle are generally clearly identifiable. One criticism that has been levelled against the operation was over the removal of modern overburdens without archaeological supervision, though it should be conceded that this was an approach taken in many quarters at that time, and the excavations did at least generally stop short of historic occupation levels. Whatever final view is taken of the work, it could never be denied that it represents an altogether remarkable achievement against considerable odds.

It is therefore in some ways rather sad to have to record that the dreams of the 45th Chief of his line to have the castle as the long-term home of his successor Chiefs of Clan Neil proved ultimately abortive. The costs of maintaining a residence at such a remote and weather-beaten castle proved to be unsupportable, and in 1996, when much that had been done was already suffering from the onslaughts of the elements, it was decided that it should be placed in the care of the state. It is now maintained by Historic Scotland.

CHAPTER 13

Stirling Castle great hall

The case of the restoration of the great hall at Stirling Castle (Fig 1.8; Fig 13.1) is an unusual one, since it involved the Ministry of Works and its successor, Historic Scotland, in the role of restorer of a monument to a previous state rather than its more usual role of conserver of monuments in their existing state. To understand why this should have been so, it is necessary to consider both the hall's significance and what had been done to it in relatively recent times.

Despite a tradition that the hall was built for James III, the building we now see was in fact an important part of a campaign by James IV to make his principal castles the backdrop to a carefully orchestrated expression of the kingship of a monarch who believed he had a place on the wider European stage, and who was also the heir to a cherished tradition of chivalry. To ensure that he was fittingly housed, the fourth James carried out major campaigns of rebuilding at many of his residences, including Edinburgh Castle, and the palaces of Linlithgow, Holyrood and Falkland, but it was at Stirling Castle that he carried out his most ambitious architectural works.

Across the main line of approach he constructed a wonderful multi-towered forework with a soaring gatehouse at its centre, which perhaps owed as much to depictions in French luxury manuscripts of castles as courts of chivalry as it did to current ideas of military defensibility. Within the forework, and on the highest point of the rock, he started work on the inner close, a great square – perhaps most appropriately described as a *cour d'honneur* – around which were to be grouped the principal buildings of the royal residence, and which archaeological investigation has shown replaced a less regular arrangement of diagonally aligned buildings. Tragically, the king's death at the battle of Flodden in 1513 almost certainly meant that his plans for Stirling were left incomplete. Nevertheless, he was able to build both his own residence, his lodging, on the west side of the close, and the great hall on the east side; he also re-established on the grandest scale the collegiate institution of the Chapel Royal of Scotland within the castle's main chapel on the north side of the close.

His lodging, in what is now known as the King's Old Building, was at the very highest point of the close, from where its windows commanded splendid views across Flanders Moss as far as the hills around Loch Lomond. It was under construction in 1496 to the design of the master masons Walter and John Merlioun. We know that the former was involved in later royal works at Dunbar castle in 1497 and the Palace of Holyrood by 1501–02, and it is evident that high-profile architects in the later Middle Ages, like their modern counterparts, might

Figure 13.1 Stirling
Castle, aerial view
(© Crown copyright)

Figure 13.2 Stirling
Castle, the hall
(© Crown copyright)

work on more than one project at any one time. Similarities of detailing between the King's Old Building and the hall may suggest that Walter and John were also the designers of the hall.

James IV built great ceremonial halls for the grandest public occasions of his monarchy at Edinburgh Castle and at Falkland Palace as well as at Stirling, but the hall at Stirling was the largest and, like so much else that was done for him at Stirling, leaves us in little doubt as to how important that castle was to him. Construction of the hall was nearing completion by 1501, when work on the wall walk was paid for, and in 1503 the walls were being plastered. Set at the lower end of the inner close, it was intended to stand out as the most prominent building within the castle as seen from the Forth valley below the castle walls, from where carvings of the king's heraldic beasts that ran along the roof ridge would have enlivened the skyline (Fig 13.1). From within the castle the hall soared above the outer close and the service courtyard to its east, though from the inner close it was less prominent because of the steeply rising ground to its west. Initially there was an open sunken area on the side towards the inner close, but in the course of the 16th century the ground levels at the eastern end of the close were raised, and the sunken area was covered over by a stone vault that left even less of the hall exposed on that side.

The main space of the hall, like the rooms within the king's lodging on the opposite side of the close, was raised above a series of barrel-vaulted chambers. Everything within the hall was directed towards making the great rectangular space overwhelmingly impressive. The chief lighting for the main body was through an upper band of clearstorey windows, which allowed rich fabrics to be hung around the lower walls, but at the high table end was a pair of projecting bay windows. Covering the space was a complex roof of hammer-beam construction, similar to that at Edinburgh Castle. Heat was supplied by no fewer than five large fireplaces, two in each of the side walls, and the fifth at the dais end behind the high table. There was a loft above the screens passage at the entrance end of the hall, and a trumpeters' gallery at the middle of the east wall. Four staircases gave access between the various levels, from the basement to the wall walk.

Many of the features of the hall, including most notably the bay windows, the hammer-beam roof and the clerestory windows, must have been new to Scotland, and it is likely that their inspiration was the great hall of the king's father-in-law, Henry VII, at Eltham Palace, near London, which had been built by Edward IV between 1479 and 1483. However, in what it would be hard to see as anything other than a piece of blatant one-upmanship, the hall at Stirling was made a little larger than that at Eltham, while the architectural vocabulary was spoken with a very Scottish dialect, so that there could be no doubt in which kingdom it was located.

The hall was to be the setting for a number of glittering occasions; but its exalted role, along with that of all the other royal palaces, greatly diminished after 1603, when James VI moved to London to take up the English crown as James I. Repairs were carried out for the 'homecomings' to Scotland of James in 1617 and of Charles I in 1633, though increasingly the castle's role was that of

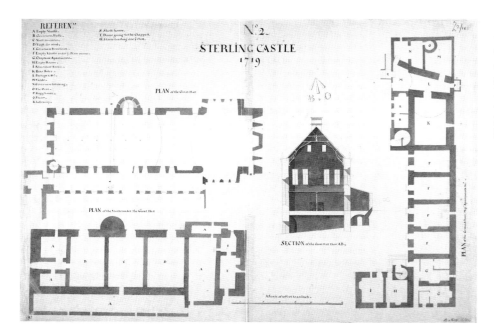

a military garrison rather than a royal residence. There are a number of survey drawings of the castle from the later 17th century onwards, and the first detailed record of the hall, which is part of a set of drawings dating from 1719, shows that by then a floor supported on posts had already been inserted along at least part of its length, while the basement was being put to mundane uses, including a stable, a brewhouse and stores for coal and wood (Fig 13.3).

The greatest change, however, took place shortly before 1800, at a time of warfare with France and North America, when there was an urgent need for additional barrack accommodation. To designs that are thought to be by John Saunders, two additional floors were inserted in the hall, together with five cross walls, between which were inserted two staircases. This operation was nothing short of architecturally devastating. The hammer-beam roof, which was by then probably in poor repair after almost two centuries of inadequate maintenance, was replaced by a very utilitarian structure, while the original windows were either destroyed or extensively modified in order to accommodate new sash windows to light each of the barrack rooms (Fig 13.4). On the west side, the central part of the outer wall, which was bulging alarmingly, was pared back in an attempt to bring it to a vertical alignment, while internally all architectural details that projected beyond the wall face were cut off. Not only were the results aesthetically disastrous, but the resultant accommodation was so poorly contrived that in 1859 an official report described it as 'the worst barracks we have seen anywhere'.

We must nevertheless be grateful that it was at least decided to retain the shell of the hall, rather than replace it by a new building. It should also be conceded that the conversion was of considerable interest for demonstrating attitudes on what was considered appropriate for barrack accommodation in the years around 1800. Nevertheless, there is no doubt that what was done greatly detracted from the architectural qualities of what had been one of Scotland's most outstanding buildings. It was perhaps particularly unfortunate – and not a little ironic – that the work was carried out at a time when interest in Scotland's medieval and Renaissance architecture was already increasing. By the mid-19th century the interest in such architecture had increased to the extent that there was a growing sense that such buildings should be actively preserved without inappropriate changes wherever possible, and, as we have already seen, the chapel within Edinburgh Castle was restored to something approaching its historic state as early as 1851 (see Fig 3.6).

So far as Stirling is concerned, the hall and adjacent palace were brought to wider attention when they were illustrated in the seminally important four-volume publication of 1845–52 by Robert William Billings, *The baronial and ecclesiastical antiquities of Scotland* (Fig 13.5). It is highly significant that the hall was not shown as it then appeared, but as Billings thought it would have looked, and in fact he was remarkably perceptive in being able to see through the alterations undergone by the bay windows to what had been originally built. Towards the end of the century, and in a spirit based on a further half-century of scholarship, David MacGibbon and Thomas Ross depicted the hall in its presumed original state in their five-volume *Castellated and domestic architecture of Scotland* of 1887–92. Here it should also be remembered that, in the year that the first of those volumes appeared, the great hall at Edinburgh Castle was restored (see Fig 3.8), and by 1893 there was a first serious proposal that the hall at Stirling should itself be similarly treated.

Pressure to restore the hall further increased after the Second World War, when the Scottish War Memorial Advisory Committee, which included James Richardson, Scotland's Inspector of Ancient Monuments, suggested that in a restored state the hall might represent a suitable memorial to those who had died in the war. Richardson went so far as to prepare a model showing how this could be done. However, the continued need for barrack accommodation within the castle, together with a sense that such a memorial might not be appropriate, meant that this was not seen as a serious option at the time.

The situation changed when the castle ceased to be a military depot in 1964. Responsibility for maintaining the buildings within the castle had in fact rested with the Office of Works since 1906, but with the change of function from an army base to what could be described as a monument, it became possible to take a more

Figure 13.4 Stirling Castle, the exterior when in use as a barrack (© Crown copyright)

historically based view of what should be done. The Office (by 1964 the Ministry)
of Works had always seen its role with regard to monuments as conserving
them in the state in which they had survived, for the value of the evidence they
embodied, rather than as restoring them to any putative earlier state. The case
of the Stirling hall, however, clearly presented difficulties for such an approach.
Whatever its academic interest might be, the barrack conversion had left a
building that had been designed as one of the Scottish kingdom's most impressive
structures in an extremely damaged state; to such an extent, indeed, that any
attempt to appreciate its original qualities required an almost impossible stretch
of the imagination for anyone who was not an architectural expert.

Taking account of this, in 1964 it was decided that investigations should be
carried out to assess the feasibility of restoration. The survey of 1719 gave a great
deal of useful information, perhaps most importantly on the form of the lost
hammer-beam roof (Fig 13.3). There could be little doubt that detailed analysis of
the evidence of the drawing, together with cross-reference to the broadly similar
roof of the hall at Edinburgh Castle (see Fig 3.8), would permit restoration of
what had been the hall's crowning glory with a high degree of accuracy (Fig 13.6).
It was also clear that there was much evidence within the surviving fabric for
the form and location of the original doorways, windows, fireplaces and stairs.
Nevertheless, much was unknown about many of the details in the existing state
of the building so it was decided that a painstaking process of archaeologically
dismantling the insertions of *c* 1800 should be undertaken, and this began in July
1964.

By 1967 it was becoming clear that there would be sufficient evidence for
some elements of restoration to be instigated, and the process of reconstructing
a number of the clearstorey windows began. One principle that was adopted
from a relatively early stage was that stonework which was damaged, but which

Figure 13.6 Stirling Castle, the hall interior (© Crown copyright)

was still capable of performing its intended structural functions, should be retained, so as to ensure that as much primary evidence as possible should be preserved for future generations. Even while some parts were being restored to their historic state, the dismantling of other parts was still taking place, and this was necessarily carried out at a very slow rate that ensured no information could be overlooked in the process. It was only as late as 1991 that it was eventually concluded there was indeed sufficient evidence for full restoration to take place, and it was decided that this should be achieved by the millennium if possible. Owing to the unpredictable nature of work of this kind there are inevitably a large number of unforeseeable factors, but happily none of those encountered in the later stages proved insuperable, and the completely restored hall was formally inaugurated by James IV's descendant, Queen Elizabeth II, on St Andrew's Day 1999. On account of the way the work of dismantling and restoration of missing features was carried out in the earlier stages, the costs had been subsumed within the general budgets of the Ministry of Works and its successors, and they cannot be identified separately. The costs of the project from 1991, however, had been in the order of £8,500,000.

There must always be questions as to whether the restoration should have been carried out, and a case can be made that the use of the hall as a barrack was as valid a part of its history as its first intended use as a setting for royal festivities. On balance, however, an exceptional response to the hall can probably be justified. On the one hand it had a unique initial significance as the focus of what was James IV's finest architectural expression of his personal kingship and of how he wished the Scottish kingdom to be regarded by the wider world. On the other hand, the hurried conversion to a barrack block had meant that no allowance was made for retention of its extraordinary architectural qualities, and the result had been a building in which aesthetic considerations had been so irrelevant that those qualities had been almost entirely obscured. As now restored, the building is as accurate a representation of its intended form as modern scholarship will permit, with as much of the evidence for the basis of the restoration exposed as possible, and with all new interventions clearly expressed. The result must therefore be allowed to speak for itself.

CHAPTER 14

Towie Barclay Castle

The tower house at Towie Barclay (Fig 1.9) is the most impressive member of a small group of closely related later 16th-century Aberdeenshire castles, of which the others are at Craig, Delgaty and Gight. An inscription on the tower proudly states that the family's founder, Sir Alexander Barclay, had died in 1136, and there are references to a castle on the site from the 14th to the 16th centuries. However, the inscription suggests that the tower only reached its present state in 1593, in the time of Sir Patrick Barclay (Fig 14.1). There has been a tradition that the master mason of this group of buildings was one Alexander Con, though there is no known documentation that would confirm this attribution.

The tower was set out to an L-shaped plan, with the main block running from south to north, and a wing projecting from the south end of the east face. The entrance, which is in the east face of the main block, immediately adjacent to the wing, opens onto a passage, rather than directly onto the stair to the upper floors

Figure 14.1 Towie Barclay Castle, the inscription recording its construction

as was more common. Immediately within the doorway is a vestibule covered by a small ribbed vault, as is also the case at Craig, Delgaty and Gight. At Towie this provides a foretaste of the altogether more splendid vaulting over the first-floor hall. The vestibule gives access to one of the vaulted basements directly ahead, and to a porter's lodge on one side. On the other side is a passage that leads to the second of the vaulted basements and to the wing, the latter originally containing the kitchen. At the end of the passage is the principal stair.

Occupying the whole of the first-floor level of the main block is the hall, a magnificent space that is covered by two bays of quadripartite ribbed vaulting carried on carved corbels, with heraldic bosses at the intersections. This vault is one of the finest examples of the revival of interest in medieval forms that is to be seen in a small number of buildings both in Scotland and England in the later 16th century. The closest Scottish parallel for the vault within a secular context is at Balbegno Castle in Kincardineshire, which dates from 1569, and

Figure 14.2 Towie Barclay Castle, the exterior before restoration (Eric Ellington)

where we are reminded that such vaults would usually have been decoratively painted.

Within the wall thickness of 2.15m, there was ample scope for the provision of a large number of mural chambers and stairs. The finest of these mural spaces is at an elevated level at the south end of the hall, where a window embrasure is treated as a carefully detailed gallery. It is covered by another miniature ribbed vault and has an altar *mensa* (slab) on its east side. This *mensa* indicates that the gallery was used as an oratory, and is a reminder that the Barclays continued to adhere to the Catholic faith after the Reformation, as did the owners of the other castles in this group. The religious affiliations of the family are also made evident in the *Arma Christi* (a heraldic depiction of the wounds of Christ) carved on the vaulting boss of the oratory, together with the symbols of the evangelists on the corbels from which the vault springs. However, both *mensa* and boss could be later insertions, and it is possible that the gallery was adapted as an oratory only at a later stage. The problems associated with adhering to the old faith in troubled times may be reflected in the slightly rueful comment incised on the inscription of 1593 on the exterior of the castle that *In tim of Valth al men semis friendly an tru frindis not knauin but in adversity* ('In prosperous times everyone seems friendly, but true friends are only known in adversity').

In 1752 the estate passed, through the marriage of Isabel, the daughter and heiress of Sir Alexander Barclay, to Charles Maitland, the second son of the Earl of Lauderdale. Although Maitland added his wife's surname to his own, he subsequently sold the estate to the Earl of Findlater, who bought it for his second son, who died soon after. The earl then sold it in 1792. It was purchased for £21,000 by the Robert Gordon's Hospital Trust, and later passed to that trust's successor body, the Aberdeen Endowments Trust. In the course of its later history the castle underwent a number of changes. The most damaging of these was in 1792, when its two upper storeys were removed to reduce it to a more manageable size, and the projection of the wing appears to have been reduced (Fig 14.2). Since then the castle has served several functions, including that of a Free Church meeting hall and an agricultural store; in 1874 it was reroofed, at which time the present parapet was built. Although it was in a declining structural state by the mid-20th century, in 1951 it was recommended for scheduling by the distinguished castle historian Douglas Simpson; this was put into effect by 1953.

In the later 1960s the present owners, Marc and Karen Ellington, became aware of the castle. They had been looking for a suitable candidate for restoration on the west coast, but fell in love with Towie Barclay which was brought to their attention by Nigel Tranter. They succeeded in acquiring it in 1969, and designs for its restoration were then sought from the Banff architect Jack Meldrum. The intention was simply to make the castle habitable in its existing truncated state, with no idea of reinstating the parts that had been removed in 1792. In 1972 a grant of £8800 was awarded from the Historic Buildings Council towards the work, and, in days when such things were still a possibility, the Council's architects and principal inspector became very closely involved in the whole project, devoting much time and even physical effort to it. These were still relatively early days in the history of modern castle restoration, and looking back on his achievement with the advantage of hindsight, Mr Ellington suspects that decisions reached on some aspects of the work might have been taken differently today. For example, the harling that was applied to the external walls was a hard cement-based mixture gauged with lime (Fig 14.3), and it was not fully appreciated at that time that both the external harling and internal plaster would have extended across the quoins and the dressed stonework framing wall openings. On a related aspect,

Figure 14.3 Towie Barclay Castle

Figure 14.4 Towie Barclay Castle, the hall before restoration (© RCAHMS. SC 1203649, Licensor www.rcahms.gov.uk)

Figure 14.5 Towie Barclay Castle, the interior of the hall (Eric Ellington)

it might not now have been decided to leave unplastered either the stonework in the entrance areas or the webbing of the hall vault, though on the latter score the absence of firm evidence as to precisely how such an important feature should be treated led to a natural sense of caution.

Whatever Mr Ellington's reservations, the results of the operation were universally deemed to be highly successful, and, as the family's collection of carefully chosen paintings and furnishings has grown, the wonderful hall has come back into its own as a space that is as much timeless as historic (Figs 14.4–14.5). In 1973 the quality of the achievement was formally recognised when the project was given both a Saltire and a Civic Trust Award. In 1975, by which time the first phase of work was complete and the castle was again habitable, it was descheduled, and statutory protection was instead afforded by its status as a listed building.

Once family life was established within the restored castle, the restrictions of living in such a building became more obvious, however. At the tower's heart is one of the most splendid great rooms in any tower house, but without the lost upper storeys there was only a small number of other rooms. It soon became clear that additional space would have to be contrived in some way. The cost of reinstating the late 16th-century upper storeys would have been prohibitive, and, in any case, there was insufficient evidence to do this in a way that could be historically based, so eventually it was decided that the new storeys should be treated as a form of extended garret, set back on the inner face of the walls of the tower's main block, and behind the 19th-century crenellated parapet. This could allow one full storey to be formed within the heightened walls, with a garret storey within the roof space (Fig 14.3). It was by no means unusual for upper storeys to be contained within walls that rose behind parapets, as may be seen over the wing at Balbegno, a castle with which Towie Barclay has much in common. While it is true that at Towie Barclay the slightly squat form of the truncated castle inevitably gave the garret a more obvious presence than would have been the case elsewhere, on balance it was probably the most appropriate means of reinstating the lost accommodation. Work was in progress to the designs of the architect Bill Cowie by 1976, and the Historic Buildings Council made a grant towards the costs of £2000.

The land initially purchased along with the tower had been quite restricted, but in the later 1980s the Ellingtons persuaded the Aberdeen Endowments Trust to sell a small steading to the north-east of the tower, along with an extent of further land. The steading consisted of an attractive grouping of three ranges of a variety of dates around a small courtyard, to one side of the main approach to the tower, one of which has been a meeting room for the Trust. It is likely that those ranges were on the site of some of the buildings that would always have been associated with the castle. The steading was restored between 1987 and 1989, with garages and outhouses being formed in the west range and the north range continuing in use as a meeting hall, while within the east range a cottage suitable for holiday letting was created. Grants of over £36,000 were given to this work by the Historic Buildings Council. Mrs Ellington, who has a professional interest in garden restoration, set about creating a formal parterre within the enclosure to the east of the tower, with a circle of box hedges framing the intersection of a cross of paths. At the southern end of the cross axis there is now a circular summer house, and a small conservatory has been located at its western end. As a result of this, the setting of the castle is now equal to the qualities of the castle itself. There is once again a sense that, as was always intended, while the tower house is the dominant element of the complex, it is no longer an isolated structure.

CHAPTER 15

Castle Menzies

As its name suggests, Castle Menzies, to the west of Aberfeldy, Perthshire (Fig 1.10), was the principal seat of the Menzies family, whose main residence before the late 15th century had been at Comrie. The present building, which is assumed to replace an earlier one on the site, was built by James Menzies and his wife Barbara, a daughter of the Earl of Atholl; the years of construction are indicated by the date 1571 inscribed on the frame of the heraldic panel above the entrance, and the date 1577 on one of the wall-head gablets.

Set out to a Z-shaped plan, it is a highly sophisticated example of domestic planning, in which the rectangular wings at diagonally opposite corners of the main block were used to ensure a high level of privacy and domestic convenience for those who occupied the various lodgings and chambers. Within the main block, which is aligned from east to west, above the barrel-vaulted chambers of the ground floor there are two principal floors and a garret, while within each of the wings, where the smaller scale of the chambers required lower ceilings, there is an additional floor. From the time it was built the castle would have been the dominant element in a matrix of courtyards, some evidence for which has been located through aerial photography. These would have provided a certain measure of added security, but their main function was to accommodate ancillary buildings and gardens, as well as to enhance the dignity and amenity of the house. The only overt tokens of defensibility in the house itself are a number of shot holes in the lower walls. There are no wall walks at the wall heads, and the roofs are contained within crow-stepped gables. In addition to the many chimney stacks, the roofline is enriched by turrets with conical roofs at several of the external angles, and also by a splendid array of richly decorated gablets to the dormer windows (Fig 15.1).

While allowance must be made for later alterations, including the provision of a new entrance and porch at the centre of the south front, it can be seen that the original entrance was at the foot of the south-west tower, where it was given greater emphasis by the heraldic panel that has been mentioned above. This opened onto a lobby with a straight flight of stairs that led on to the spiral stair at the north-west corner of the south-west wing. The entrance also gave access to a corridor that ran alongside the vaulted compartments of the ground floor, the easternmost of which was the kitchen. The ground floor was modified in the 18th century, when the new entrance was created, opening on to a vestibule leading through to a more spacious stair to the rear; several of the other chambers at this level were then fitted out for domestic functions.

At first-floor level about two-thirds of the main block was taken up by the hall (Fig 15.2), with what was probably the principal lodging at its eastern end, the

Figure 15.1 Castle Menzies

latter consisting of an outer chamber in the main block and an inner chamber in the wing, with closets leading off both. The south-west wing at this level evidently housed a lesser lodging of a chamber and closet. The planning of the second floor of the main block has been modified on a number of occasions. By analogy with other houses of around this date that show a similar level of sophistication, such as Elcho in Perthshire, it is likely that the space corresponding to the hall on the floor below would initially have been subdivided into two rooms by a timber partition, as suggested by the positioning of the two fireplaces. But by around the 1660s it can be seen from the ceiling with the initials of Sir Alexander Menzies and his wife that it was treated as single space, perhaps functioning as a gallery, with a lodging to the east like that on the first floor.

Further works were in progress in 1738–39, when payments were made to various craftsmen. It is likely that this related to internal refitting and to the creation of the entrance vestibule and the addition of the new stair to the north of the main block that has already been mentioned. Eventually the additions on the north side of the house extended the length of the main block and rose to its full height. Also around the 1730s, relatively low-key additions were made to the service courtyards on the north side of the house, with a one-and-a-half-storey range projecting from the north-east corner likely to date from around then.

The most extensive changes, however, were those carried out for Sir Neil Menzies by William Burn in 1836–39. As might be expected from an architect who was to become the greatest exponent of the effective planning of service and family accommodation at country houses, much of his work was concerned with additions to the servants' quarters, while a large new wing for the family was added to the west of the main body of the house. Early views show that there was already a corridor to the west of the house before Burn started work, and this was retained as part of the new arrangements for internal communication. The earliest drawings for the new west wing date from 1836 (Fig 15.3), but the final scheme, with

Figure 15.2 Castle
Menzies, the hall

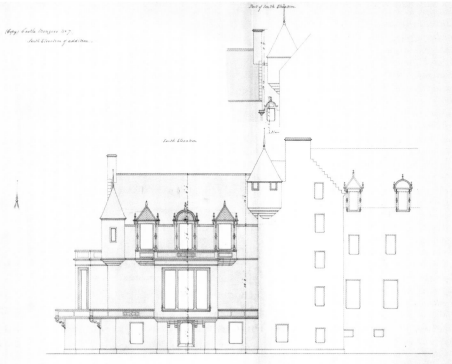

Figure 15.3 Castle
Menzies an early
proposal for the west
wing by William
Burn (© RCAHMS
(William Burn
Collection). DP
078387, Licensor
www.rcahms.gov.uk)

four storeys of accommodation, was not agreed until 1839. The principal element was a drawing room, later known as the ballroom, on the first floor. There were servants' rooms, together with what was probably Sir Neil's office on the ground floor; the family bedroom suite was on the second floor, with nurseries above that. Burn's work at Castle Menzies came at a very early stage in the development of the architect's understanding of 'baronial' architecture, and it is significant that it predates the publication of Billings' *Baronial and ecclesiastical antiquities* of 1845–52. While Burn certainly made every effort to take his lead from the late 16th-century castle for most of the details of his work, it should probably be conceded that the results have a slightly attenuated appearance that indicates a less sure hand than is to be found in his later works in this idiom. But that in itself gives the wing a particular interest for the understanding of Burn's career.

Castle Menzies remained the home of the family that had built it until the main line died out in 1918, and it was subsequently put to a number of unsuitable uses. During the Second World War it served as a hospital for Polish forces, but after this its condition declined dramatically, and the view eventually emerged in the 1950s that there was little alternative to demolition. To understand this, it is important to remember that the period after the war was a time of great financial austerity when there seemed to be little hope for large numbers of country houses. Many had been left in a devastated condition as a result of rough treatment during war-time requisitioning, and there was virtually no prospect of the life they represented being revived, particularly since there was scant hope of either recruiting or paying for the large numbers of servants required to run such houses. As a result, growing numbers of great houses were being demolished, and it was hardly surprising that this should have been proposed for Castle Menzies. However, in order to ensure that this could not happen without due consideration of all the implications, following a visit by the government's Inspector of Ancient Monuments in 1955, it was eventually recommended in 1958 that it should be scheduled as a monument of national importance, and this was eventually put into effect in 1960.

By then there had also been a positive development, because in 1957 the castle was acquired by the Clan Menzies Society, whose aspiration was to restore it as a base for the clan's activities. The castle's future was thus looking rather more hopeful. Nevertheless, preservation of such a major complex of buildings represented a massive challenge, and, at a time when Victorian architecture was generally regarded with distaste, the initial priority was to preserve no more than the 16th-century core of building. Consequently, as the clan society began to gather together resources and seek a way forward, it was assumed that almost everything apart from the original building would be demolished. By the early 1970s, however, under the dynamic leadership of the clan society's activities by Dr and Mrs A D Dewar, and when it was becoming possible to contemplate initiating the first major works, somewhat more conservative attitudes were also emerging. While there was little prospect of preserving all of the derelict 18th- and 19th- century additions in a complete state, it was now seen as worth considering that parts of them should at least be preserved as roofless shells.

In 1970, Historic Scotland's architects costed works on that basis at £7000 for the most urgent requirements and at £40,000 for the longer-term needs. The architect A L McMullen was engaged to draw up proposals, though by the time the first works were instigated in 1972 the costs had risen dramatically, and between 1972 and 1975 the Historic Buildings Council gave grants of £18,200 towards just the first stage of works on the main body of the castle.

It was becoming increasingly clear, however, that it would not be possible to retain even the shell of all of the 18th- and 19th-century service ranges to the rear of the castle within the resources likely to be available, and in 1976 most of these were demolished. The only exception was a range that projected behind the west wing, which was adapted as a warden's flat and visitors' lavatories. In all this time the fate of Burn's west wing still hung in the balance, and with nothing being done to maintain it, its condition was deteriorating. When a further application for grant assistance was submitted to the Historic Buildings Council in 1980 it was recommended by the Council's Inspector that the wing was of considerable historic and architectural interest and should be retained, even though the estimated costs of doing so were in excess of £225,000. After a period of consideration and further gathering of funds, grant assistance was sought for this in 1985, and over the following years it was brought back into a sound state. The architects for much of this were William Cadell, and later the Pollock Hammond Partnership, which continued Cadell's architectural practice.

The clan society's work on the castle has involved both conservation and restoration. Much of the basement of the main building, and also the roof space, have been left in a stripped out but structurally stabilised condition. Elsewhere the aim has been to revert to a historic appearance, and a number of rooms have been furnished with paintings and furniture, some of which originated in the house. The greatest single effort of non-structural restoration was in the principal room on the second floor, where the damaged panelling was restored and missing parts of the 17th-century plaster ceiling were reinstated. Elsewhere, as in the hall and chamber in the main building and the drawing room in the west wing, much of the most visible work has been essentially decorative, with the aim of giving a sense of the likely appearance of those rooms in the 18th or 19th centuries (Fig 15.2). The castle is now an active tourist attraction, a focus for the worldwide interest of clan members, and a popular venue for events such as weddings and corporate receptions. There has thus been a remarkable transformation from the 1950s, when it was assumed that demolition was almost inevitable. Although there have been many difficulties on the way, a great deal of credit is due to the bodies and individuals who had the vision to see that there was a future for the castle when so many similar buildings were being lost. It may be mentioned that by the time work had brought the remaining parts of the castle to a structurally sound state, the Historic Buildings Council had given grants totalling in excess of £254,000.

CHAPTER 16

Balgonie Castle

The lands of Balgonie, Fife, were in the possession of the Sibbald family from perhaps as early as the mid-13th century, though nothing survives above ground from as far back as then (Fig 1.11). The earliest part of what is now seen, and the dominant feature of the castle as a whole, is a rectangular ashlar-built tower house that is usually dated to the early 15th century, though the details and planning suggest that a later 14th-century date could be as likely (Fig 16.1). It rises through five storeys, including the basement and garret, with a stair within the wall thickness at the north-east corner interconnecting the floors above the basement. Both the basement and first floor are covered by barrel vaults, and there were entrances at each of those levels, with the only internal access between the two by way of a hatch through the lower vault. The hall is likely to have been at first-floor level, and its heating must have been provided from a central hearth or brazier. There were chambers in the two floors above, each of which was provided with a fireplace; both were also provided with a latrine corbelled out towards the west end of the north side, though the way in which one is placed directly over the other must have had certain negative consequences for waste disposal. The garret and wall walk appear likely to date from a 16th-century reconstruction. Those uppermost elements of a tower were generally built with the thinnest walls while also being the most exposed to the onslaughts of the elements, and they were thus the parts most likely to require rebuilding. At the same time they were also the parts of a tower that were most prominently visible, and therefore most likely to be modified in response to changing architectural fashions.

An important part of Balgonie's value is its completeness as a group that demonstrates the architectural response to the expanding domestic needs and the increasingly high social standing of its occupants. Excavations in 1978 located traces of earlier buildings within the south-eastern area of the courtyard

Figure 16.1 Balgonie Castle, the tower house

Figure 16.2 Balgonie
Castle, the north and
east ranges

which suggest there had originally been a less regular – and perhaps less impressive – arrangement of ancillary buildings than is now seen. In the course of the 15th, 16th, 17th and early 18th centuries, however, new and more architecturally imposing ranges of residential buildings were extended outwards from the tower. The most substantial of these were set out along the northern and eastern edges of the quadrangular courtyard, the principal entrance to which was in the west wall of the courtyard, through a gatehouse with a single drum tower that is likely to be of later 16th-century date. The resultant group represents one of the most complete examples of a particularly Scottish approach to high-status domestic planning.

The earliest of the additions to have survived in identifiable form is the range on the north side of the courtyard (Fig 16.2), to the east of the tower, which possibly incorporated an existing courtyard wall on its north side. This range appears to have contained a lodging in the usual form of a hall and chamber at first-floor level, above barrel-vaulted cellars. The likelihood that the chamber was at the far end of the range from the tower suggests that the tower was no longer the location of any of the principal accommodation, though the prestige its prominence continued to afford to the castle as a whole would have more than justified the tower's retention. The surviving details of the hall and chamber range would be consistent with a date around 1496, when a royal gift to masons is recorded; the castle's owner at that time was Sir Robert Lundie, who was Lord High Treasurer of Scotland. There could be some work of a similar date as the hall and chamber range in the barrel-vaulted basement of the range at the south-east corner of the courtyard, since a window there has mouldings similar to one in the basement of the hall range.

Next in date after the north range is the main body of that at the south-east corner of the courtyard, which has been extensively modified at a number of dates. The principal phase of building is datable to between about 1635 and 1641 on the evidence of an armorial plaque that used to be there: that plaque related to Sir Alexander Leslie, who acquired the estate at a date between 1632 and 1635, and who was elevated to the earldom of Leven in 1641. There was also armorial decoration on a plaster ceiling within the range until relatively recently.

Various modifications were made to the hall and chamber range in the 17th century, when an extra storey was added. Parts of this work probably date from 1666, when it is known that the master mason John Mylne was employed at the castle, during the time that the estates were held by a daughter of the second Earl of Leven. However, much of the work on the range must have been done some decades later.

Between the north and south-east ranges is a building which now has all the appearance of being an infill block. This can probably be associated in its present form with work carried out in the first decade of the 18th century by the mason Gilbert Smith, and certainly the bolection-type mouldings of the fireplaces throughout this building, and the positioning of the windows immediately beneath the wall-head cornice, are consistent with an early 18th-century date. But there are some indications that the block could have occupied the site of an earlier and narrower range, perhaps in the form of a gallery interconnecting the north range and the range at the south-east corner. There may have been further work on the north range around the same time that the south-east range was built to its present form, with the internal subdivisions being modified to create a series of more intimate chambers. Smaller bolection-moulded fireplaces like those in the south-east range were inserted within the earlier fireplace openings, and to provide more stately access a handsome stone scale-and-platt stair was added in an offshoot at the north range's junction with the tower.

The result of all these changes would have been an extended sequence of fine rooms running at first- and second-storey levels through both the north and east ranges, with access from the stair at the west end of the north range. The tower must still have continued in use of some kind, however, since new doorways were cut through to its first and second floors from the new stair. There was also eventually a south range outside the courtyard wall, though this may have been a relatively late augmentation.

At least some of the buildings of the castle remained habitable into the last century, with improvements being carried out in 1755 for the eighth Earl of Leven. By the middle of the following century, however, after the estate had passed to the Balfours of Whittingehame, the greater part of the castle was said to be falling into decay. Nevertheless, the south-east range continued to be occupied into the 20th century, and some work was also carried out on the tower house, since in about 1912 a concrete floor supported by girders was inserted above its principal chamber.

Although the castle was scheduled as an ancient monument in 1936, its condition continued to decline over the ensuing decades. The first positive sign of hope came in 1969, when the Glenrothes Development Corporation expressed an interest in restoring the castle as an amenity for the new town, which was rapidly expanding towards Balgonie. However, in 1971 Mr David Maxwell said he was in the process of buying the castle, with a view to restoring the tower house for his own occupation. First plans for doing this were drawn up by the architect and historian George Hay, who estimated the likely costs at £45,850, and the Historic Buildings Council for Scotland was asked about the possibility of grant assistance. Unfortunately, George Hay's declining health meant he was unable to continue his involvement, and in 1973 Bill Murray Jack, of Cunningham Jack Fisher Purdom Architects was appointed in his place; he estimated the costs of restoring the tower house at £52,595. By that time Fife Regional Council, which had taken over responsibility for Glenrothes, was considering the restoration of the courtyard buildings for arts and community use.

Work was advancing well on the consolidation and reroofing of the tower house for Mr Maxwell by the mid-1970s, with a grant of £14,000 from the Historic Buildings Council, and a grant together with an interest-free loan from Fife Council. The restoration of the tower house presented relatively few problems of accuracy, since the shell had survived well; the principal loss was the parapet of the wall walk, and a decision had to be taken on what should be done to reinstate this in 1976. From the surviving structural evidence it was clear that, as might be expected, in its final form the parapet had been projected out on corbels, with rounds at the corners, but there was no physical evidence for the height of the parapet or for the form of the crenellation. Fortunately, since the loss of the parapet had been fairly recent, there were a number of illustrations that recorded its final state, including photographs in the Royal Commission on the Ancient and Historical Monuments of Scotland's *Inventory of Fife*, which had been published as recently as 1933. It was therefore possible to reinstate the parapet with a high level of accuracy (Fig 16.1). A slightly surprising feature was that it had risen to a relatively low height, suggesting that its purpose had been very much more decorative than functional.

By 1976 Fife Council had decided that they would be unable to assume responsibility for the courtyard buildings, and it was agreed that the open area of the courtyard should be simply landscaped. Since this would involve the lowering of ground surfaces, Historic Scotland required that this should be done under archaeological supervision. It was accepted that this was to be carried out as a Job Creation Project under the direction of Dr Nick Dixon, and Historic Scotland provided a grant of £1148 in 1977 to cover the costs, with a further grant of £600 towards post-excavation work in the following year. The archaeological investigations proved to be of great interest for the information that they provided on the earlier arrangement of some buildings within the south-eastern corner of the courtyard. These indicated that there had once been at least a partial south range within the present limits of the courtyard, and that there had been an earlier building on an oblique alignment within the south-east corner of the courtyard. All of this suggested that at the earlier stages of its development the courtyard had been considerably less spacious and regularly disposed than was eventually the case.

The year 1978 saw an extended pause in the ongoing restoration of the tower house due to the illness of the stone mason who was leading the operation. Nevertheless, by 1979 it was possible to mark the completion of the first phase

Figure 16.3 Balgonie Castle, the hall in the tower house

of work with a celebration, and by that stage the tower was in a wind- and water-tight condition. Payment of the final instalment of the Historic Buildings Council grant was made in 1981. Unfortunately, by that stage, Mr Maxwell was coming to realise that, for personal reasons, he would be unable to live in the tower once it was completed, and with great reluctance he decided he had to place it on the market.

In 1985 it was announced that Mr and Mrs Raymond Morris and their son Stuart had bought the castle. They immediately set about completing enough of the work on the tower to make it habitable, even though it proved to be dauntingly cold in the winter months. As part of this work, the missing steps of the 17th-century scale-and-platt stair were replaced in timber rather than the original stone, while the first-floor hall was fitted out with a screen and gallery, albeit of slightly reduced proportions from what was probably originally there. The upper floors of the tower are now used by the Morris family as their living quarters. By 1987 their thoughts had moved on to the possibility of restoring the courtyard ranges, and they commissioned Cunningham Jack Fisher Purdom Architects to draw up proposals for this, which were costed at £556,000. Unfortunately, it has not yet been possible to take this beyond making the basement of the north range secure from the elements. The Morris family continue to show great commitment to the castle, and Stuart Morris has completed a degree in heritage management in order to ensure that he is well qualified to manage the castle as effectively as possible. They have now built up a successful business in hosting weddings, with a chapel and ante-chapel in the barrel-vaulted central and eastern rooms of the north range basement, while the hall in the tower can be used for receptions (Fig 16.3). They still have hopes for full restoration of the courtyard ranges.

CHAPTER 17

Rossend Castle

Rossend Castle (Fife) is at Burntisland, which was earlier known as Wester Kinghorn (Fig 1.12); the name Rossend may itself be no earlier than the 18th century. The castle overlooks the harbour, which was to be a principal source of income for its occupants until the later 19th century. It is a large T-shaped building (Fig 17.1) consisting of a west range that is aligned from west to east, and forms the stem of the T, and an east range that is aligned from south to north, and forms the head of the T. Those ranges achieved their final form as a consequence of a complex, and still only partly comprehensible, sequence of developments.

Before the Reformation the castle and associated estates had been a possession of the abbey of Dunfermline, and the oldest elements of the present building probably date from the time that the site was occupied by a manor house of the abbots. Those earliest parts appear to be the south and west walls of the west range, which rise from a substantial moulded base course, and there have been three small lancet windows at ground-floor level of the south wall (17.2). It has been suggested that these walls belonged to an abbatial chapel, though it is perhaps as likely that they formed part of the undercroft of the abbot's hall.

By 1554 the head of Dunfermline Abbey, the commendator George Drury, had transferred the estate to his illegitimate son, Peter, in order to provide him with an inheritance. It was presumably he who started construction of the east range, set at right angles to the earlier building, perhaps to provide a more commodious

Figure 17.1
Rossend Castle

lodging for himself as an extension of the existing hall. The new work is probably datable to 22 May 1554 on the evidence of a relocated inscription and a shield with the arms of Drury, while on the east wall there are the arms that came to be associated with St Margaret, the founder of the Benedictine community at Dunfermline. The ground floor of the new range was divided into two barrel-vaulted compartments. At first-floor level it seems there was a lodging consisting of a hall and chamber, and it is possible that the hall rose to a greater height than the chamber, though the later changes that the castle has undergone make it difficult to be certain of that. In its present state there are two floors above the level of the hall, but the range may have been heightened on more than one occasion, and initially it possibly consisted of no more than the ground and first floors.

After passing through a number of hands, the castle and estates were granted to Sir Robert Melville by Mary Queen of Scots; despite being forfeited for a while, they were restored to him in 1587. Melville appears to have carried out major works on both ranges, albeit with the greatest concentration of effort on the east range. At least one additional storey is thought to have been added to that range in his time, and it was evidently extended a short way to the north to accommodate a new kitchen fireplace at basement level, with a flue rising through the north end of the similarly extended upper storeys. To the north-west it was probably Melville who added a new entrance at the foot of a stair tower inserted into the northern re-entrant angle between the two ranges. In the course of that work, two ceilings were given painted decoration. One of those, which survives only as a number of fragments, was decorated with heraldry. The other, which was over the first-floor hall of the east range, has complex decoration including

Figure 17.2 Rossend Castle, the earlier work along the south wall of the west range

a number of rather enigmatic symbols, which can be dated from the presence of Sir Robert Melville's initials to between 1587 and 1621. It is possible that it was painted in time for the Scottish 'homecoming' of James VI and I in 1617, at which time Melville was ordered by the Privy Council to prepare the castle for a royal visit. It was perhaps as an extension of the same operation that a handsome new state apartment was formed above inserted ground-floor vaulting at first-floor level of the west range. As might be expected at this time, this probably consisted of a hall and chamber, with a screened-off vestibule and servery area at the east end that could be accessed from the new stair at the junction of the two blocks.

Amongst later changes for which there is some evidence, a gablet on the north face of the west range bears the date 1665, indicating that work was being carried out when it was in the ownership of General James Wemyss. But from this stage onwards it becomes very difficult to be certain of the precise building sequence, since there are traces of many additions and alterations of a relatively minor structural nature, some of which have been wholly or partly obscured by yet further changes. At some stage, possibly in the earlier 18th century, the west range was augmented by a low building running the length of its north flank (Fig 17.3). However, much of the work carried out in the later years of the 17th century and the early years of the 18th was directed towards fitting out the more important interiors with fine panelling. Some of that panelling was of softwood that was intended to be painted, but in the more important rooms it was of oak in which the exposed and polished grain was intended to be seen to advantage. It is particularly regrettable that none of this survives in place.

Further works were carried out in the early 19th century. The date 1816 was inscribed on the outbuildings, and the initials ESB associated with that date presumably refer to Major General Edward Swift Broughton, the owner at that time. It was perhaps around then that the building added against the north face of the west range was heightened and capped by a crenellated parapet to give the entrance front of the house a more castellated appearance (Fig 17.4). Possibly in the same years the southern end of the east range was raised by a further storey,

Figure 17.3 Rossend Castle, the plan in its latest habitable state (MacGibbon and Ross)

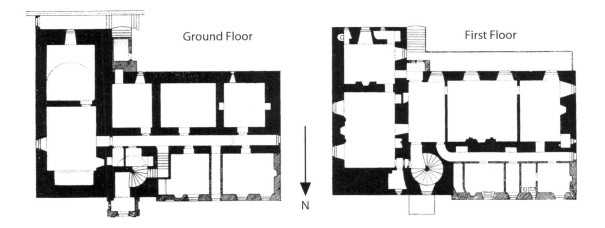

Ground Floor

First Floor

N

and that was also capped by a crenellated parapet. From this added storey there were fine views over the harbour, still one of the main sources of income of the castle's occupants.

In 1875 the castle and harbour were bought by Burntisland Town Council, though the castle itself was then sold on to James Shepherd. It was reacquired by the Council in 1907 and was for many years afterwards used as a boarding house, a function that continued until 1946, after which it was used as a store by the Burntisland Shipping Company. This latter function itself ceased in 1952, and the condition of the castle then began to decline rapidly, largely as a consequence of high levels of vandalism. Some of the fine panelling in the best rooms, which was already damaged, was removed and reset in the modern 'castle' of Easterheughs, which was built by William R Thomas on the outskirts of Burntisland between 1946 and 1955. In 1955 the Town Council, which was coming to feel that the deteriorating condition of such a prominently sited building was reflecting no credit on the burgh, offered it into the guardianship of the state. When this was found not to be possible the Council decided that it should be demolished. Extended but somewhat sporadic discussions followed, during which a stone fell through the upper floors of the east range. While this was certainly a disaster, there was the silver lining that one of the painted ceilings that had been installed by Sir Robert Melville, but that had been concealed by a later plaster ceiling, was revealed (Fig 17.5). Since there was at the time no prospect of conserving the ceiling while it remained in place, it was removed to the National Museum of Scotland, and is now displayed within the museum.

In 1960, the Secretary of State for Scotland was persuaded by Burntisland Council that there was little prospect of finding a new use for the castle and he agreed that it could be demolished. However, finding a way of doing this at a reasonable cost proved to be a more difficult task than had been anticipated, since the Territorial Army, the Royal Engineers and the Royal Navy all declined to undertake the work. A further decade of continuing decline followed, but by 1970 the Town Council decided that demolition must take place, and once again the Secretary of State's permission was sought to do this. By then, however, there was a growing body of opinion at both local and national level that the castle was simply too important to be lost. At the last moment, when a demolition crew was already on site, permission to demolish was withdrawn, and the castle was listed at category B. In 1971 a Public Local Inquiry was held into the Council's application to demolish the castle, and the Reporter at the Inquiry recommended that the Secretary of State should not grant permission.

A number of proposals for restoration and reuse were then put forward. Already by 1970 the architects Wheeler and Sproson had drawn up a scheme to create fifteen apartments at a cost of £81,358, but when in the following year the Link Housing Association put forward proposals for subdivision they were thwarted by the Council's refusal to provide the grant assistance that might have been expected for such work. By 1973 nothing had yet been achieved, and the Council once again applied for permission to demolish. In response to this, a meeting of all interested parties was convened in the following year under the aegis of the Scottish Development Department. It was at this stage that Ian Begg said that his firm of architects was prepared to buy the castle in order restore it as its own headquarters. Purchase was finally agreed in 1975 for the nominal sum of £350; the purchasers were Ian Begg and Larry Rolland for the partnership of Robert Hurd and Partners and L A Rolland and Partners, which later became the Hurd Rolland Partnership. The initial estimated project costs were £54,500.

Figure 17.5 Rossend Castle, the interior after a fall of stone revealed the painted ceiling (© RCAHMS. SC 1203673, Licensor www.rcahms.gov.uk)

Once detailed designs had been drawn up by Ian Begg and Larry Rolland, initial progress was rapid. As a first stage the building was made wind- and water-tight, with the Historic Buildings Council for Scotland giving a 60% grant of £18,000 towards this phase in 1976. As investigation of the building's structural condition was completed it was decided that it would be very difficult to retain the narrow range that had been added against the north face of the west range. Although greater efforts might now be made to retain it for its value as a part of the building's complex architectural history, in the conservation climate of the time this was felt to be an acceptable loss, since relatively little value was as yet placed on 19th-century work. By 1978 internal reinstatement was in progress, and the Historic Buildings Council gave a 39% grant of £22,000 towards this, with a further 39% grant of £23,000 in 1983.

In general the aim of the work was to take the building back to a state as close as possible to that it had assumed by the 17th century, though the intended use of the building as an office meant that some compromises had to be made. The need for large office spaces and heavy loadings, for example, called for joists of reinforced steel rather than of timber to be inserted in a number of areas. There were also difficulties resulting from the fact that in some parts there was insufficient evidence for the building's 17th-century state because of the later changes that had been made. Consequently, at first-floor level of the west range, where there were three rooms by the later 19th century, it was decided to treat that level as a single space. As has already been said, we might now conclude that it was more likely that in the 17th century it had been set out as an apartment consisting of a hall and chamber, but in the 1970s there had been little research into medieval and Renaissance planning. For some of the other principal rooms the previous removal of the painted ceilings and panelling made full restoration unachievable but, as some compensation, panelling from Polton House, which was itself to be demolished, was acquired and was installed in the chamber at the south end of the east range.

In the central decades of the 20th century there was a strong sense that, even in dealing with historic buildings, it was important that there should be some overt expression of the period at which the work was being carried out, and that not to do this would be essentially dishonest. As part of the restoration process at Rossend, it was therefore felt appropriate to add a small number of modern touches in order to demonstrate that the act of bringing the castle back into use was itself a part of its ongoing history. Amongst these additions was a tubular fire escape stair projecting from the west gable of the west range, which is now largely hidden within the trees on that side of the castle. A rather more visible addition was a tent roof with a glazed gable over the 19th-century flat terrace at the south end of the east range, which continued the roof line of the northern part of the range. This is a feature that is particularly prominent in distant views of the castle, and that is given strong individual expression through the use of slate rather than tile for its covering. The adoption of such a design is distinctly a product of the climate of thought of the time at which the work was carried out, and it is of some interest on that account. Nevertheless, one suspects that, if the restoration were being carried out today, it is not something that would be proposed.

Once the essential work that permitted the castle to be brought into use had been finished, the final fitting out was completed at a more leisurely rate, and was still in progress as late as 1988. It had been possible to see what the results would be for some years before then, however, and these were met with widespread and fully justified acclaim. In 1982 this was recognised when the Royal Incorporation of Architects awarded the work its first prize in the Urban Conservation Projects category. It says much for the way the work was planned and carried out that it has continued in the use for which it was restored in the 1970s with very few modifications being required.

CHAPTER 18

Aikwood Tower

Aikwood Tower (or Oakwood Tower as it has tended to be known more recently), Selkirkshire, is on record from at least the mid-15th century (Fig 1.13). By the early 16th century, it was the residence of a branch of the Scott family, and there are references to a tower being there by 1541, but in its present form the tower is clearly for the most part later than that. What is now seen is assumed to have been built by Robert Scott, with the likely year of construction recorded on a voussoir incised with his initials and the date 1602, which was reset over a doorway on the south face of the tower.

Externally the tower is a large but seemingly very simple rectangular structure (Fig 18.1). The rubble walls are pierced by randomly disposed small windows with a variety of mouldings to their reveals, which may suggest that some have been reused from an earlier building on the site. The round-arched entrance, which is in the north face, is framed by heavy double-roll mouldings, and there is a wide-mouthed shot hole to its left. At the wall head there is no wall walk or parapet, and the roof is contained above the side walls by crow-stepped gables. A lighter note was introduced by a pair of gableted dormers on both the north and south faces to light the third floor, while at the north-west and the south-east corners are small box-like cap houses projected out on enriched corbelling, each with a small crow-stepped gable. Additional openings have been cut through the basement walls for agricultural purposes after the tower was no longer lived in, including a wide cart opening in the east face.

Internally, there were three storeys over a barrel-vaulted basement, though the top-floor level was modified when the tower was in agricultural use. The

Figure 18.1 Aikwood Tower

entrance opens onto a short passage, from which there were doorways into both of the two compartments of the basement; the passage also leads to the spiral stair at the north-west corner that interconnects all of the floors. In contrast to the external simplicity, the planning of the tower is unexpectedly complex in the way that both the first and second floors are divided into a larger and a lesser room, with separate access to each of them from the stair. The two rooms on the first

Figure 18.2 Aikwood Tower, the interior of the hall

and second floors have their own fireplaces, that in the larger of the two rooms on the first floor, which was presumably the hall, being particularly impressive: it has filleted-roll jambs and a corbelled-out segmental joggled arch (Fig 18.2). At second-floor level the larger room, which was almost certainly the owner's chamber, had its own stool closet, whereas at first-floor level it is the smaller chamber that has a stool closet.

The tower continued to be occupied into the early 18th century, and in 1722 it was said to be surrounded by orchards and gardens, though it soon afterwards became the house associated with a tenanted farm on the Polwarth estate. In c 1800 a new farmhouse was built in the form of a range against the tower's south face, though by the middle of the 19th century a more commodious farmhouse had been built nearby, and the tower and south range were adapted for the agricultural uses that have already been mentioned. This adaptation ensured that both the tower and range continued to survive in a structurally complete and roofed state. After the Second World War the farm passed into the ownership of the Buccleuch estate. In 1955 the estate enquired about the possibility of government assistance towards remedial works on the tower, though in the harsh economic climate of the times there was little prospect of state funds being found for any but the most outstanding monuments. It was only in 1970 that the significance of the tower was recognised sufficiently for it to be scheduled as a monument of national importance.

In the early 1970s David and Judy Steel (the future Lord and Lady Steel of Aikwood) began to take an interest in the tower. Their concern for its declining condition led them to write to the eighth Duke of Buccleuch, and to air the possibility of its restoration, but the duke felt there would be difficulties in having a restored tower at the heart of a working farm. After the ninth duke succeeded in 1973 there was a change of attitude, though by then David Steel's responsibilities as leader of the Liberal and later of the Liberal Democrat party meant there was little possibility of his undertaking restoration at that time. It was only once he had resigned the leadership in 1988 that he once again began to think of doing so. With the encouragement of his wife, matters moved swiftly, and later that year the purchase was agreed, and discussions were opened with Historic Scotland and other interested parties on how to take this forward.

The tower at Aikwood offered a number of features which made it more suitable for restoration for modern occupation than many other houses of its period of construction. In the first place, it was structurally complete and generally in sound condition, apart from the need to reinstate the top floor at its original level and to carry out repairs to the roof. In the second place, its planning – with two rooms to each of the main floors – meant that it was likely to be easier to live in than many towers with just one room to each floor. And thirdly, the juxtaposition of the earlier farmhouse to the south, that had been adapted to serve as a byre, provided space for additional functions that could not be accommodated within the tower itself (see Fig 11.4).

In 1989 there were preliminary discussions with the architect William Cadell, and his partner Malcolm Hammond (subsequently of the Pollock Hammond Partnership) was soon afterwards appointed project architect. Once momentum had been established, detailed proposals for the restoration were drawn up, costed at £256,600, towards which the Historic Buildings Council for Scotland offered grants totalling £62,000. There was some difficulty in finding a contractor to undertake the whole of the restoration project, and it was decided that individual tradesmen should be appointed for each aspect of the work.

The initial intention had been to locate the kitchen within the byre, in the part immediately next to the tower. But when it was decided that a large opening that had been cut for agricultural carts in the east wall of the tower should be retained (see Fig 11.4), it was seen that the eastern compartment of the basement would lend itself very well to use as a kitchen and dining room, with a cloakroom and space for storage in the smaller western compartment. At first-floor level, the spacious hall, with its generously proportioned fireplace, lent itself naturally to use as a drawing room (Fig 18.2), with a more intimate sitting room in the western compartment. The principal bedroom was located at second-floor level, with a handsome bathroom created in the adjacent space. The third floor rises up into the roof space, where it is lit by dormer windows. It had been initially assumed that there would be space for only one level of rooms within the roof, as had certainly been the case when the tower was built. However, when the floor at this top level was lowered to its original line, it was decided that two floors of bedrooms could be accommodated, each with its own bathroom. This had the disadvantage that the roof collars at fourth-floor level had to be raised within the bedroom to give sufficient headroom (see Fig 11.1), though this could be avoided in the corridor that led up to the bedroom and the bathroom to its side.

Certain aspects of the external detailing of the tower were a matter of discussion. David Steel had seen a number of restored towers where he felt that the introduction of rainwater goods had detracted from the appearance, and he wished to avoid this at Aikwood, so it was decided that the rainwater should be allowed simply to run off the roof, as would have been the case when it was built. The treatment of the walls themselves has perhaps been more problematic. The external masonry of towers like that at Aikwood would invariably have been covered by a lime render, and many tower house restorers have chosen to reinstate that finish. The difficulty lies in doing so in a way that is historically accurate, and it can be argued that, if this cannot be achieved, it is misleading to introduce an inappropriate finish. The advice that Historic Scotland gave was that, if an external render were to be applied, it should be based on the most careful analysis of any surviving evidence, but that there would be no objection if it was decided not to reapply a render, particularly since it would be possible to do this at a later stage if it was decided to be in the tower's long-term interest. After careful consideration, the Steels decided not to apply a render. It has to be said that there have been some minor problems of water ingress through the walls, particularly through the thinner masonry of chimney flues, and there have been thoughts of rendering in the hope that this might prevent further penetration, though this has so far not been done.

Restoration of Aikwood was well advanced by 1990, though the finishing touches were still in progress two years later. It had been intended that work on the byre would be postponed for some years, but in the event it was carried forward more quickly than initially proposed. At the lower level of the byre a hall that can also be used for exhibitions and theatrical events was formed, while within the roof space is a library and office. That upper level can be reached either by a modern stair within the byre itself, or by a doorway from the hall of the tower.

When work was being planned at Aikwood, the initial approach was to take the tower back to its early 17th-century state, reversing all of the agricultural modifications, but, as discussion progressed, it came to be seen that some of the agricultural adaptations were not only a part of the building's history, but that their retention would make it easier to adapt it for modern occupation. In particular, the openings that had been cut through to the byre from the tower made access between the two parts more workable, while, as has been mentioned, the wide arched opening through the east wall of the tower allowed an attractive level of light into the basement that would be lost if it were to be infilled. In conservation terms, the ideal approach in circumstances of this kind is to be completely consistent, meaning that the final state of the tower should be accepted in all respects, but it is seldom possible to be fully consistent.

As one example of the difficulties complete consistency would have presented, in order to adapt the tower for agricultural use, the access to the east compartment of the basement from the stair had been blocked when the wide door was cut through the end wall, but to retain that blocking would have made the use of the basement very difficult. It was therefore agreed that it could be removed. An even greater problem would have had to be faced at the third-floor level, where the floor itself had been raised in a way that detracted from the spatial qualities of both the second- and third-floor rooms, and that left a number of features with a plainly non-historic appearance. Inevitably, therefore, there had to be some compromises. Despite those difficulties, it has been possible to respect the character and history of the tower to a very high degree, and the result has been the creation of a home that is easy – and highly attractive – to live in.

CHAPTER 19

Liberton Tower

Liberton Tower, Midlothian, was the residence of the Dalmahoy family of Over (or Upper) Liberton, and was probably built for them not long after 1453, when they are thought to have acquired the estate (Fig 1.14). It rises through two principal stages, each of which is subdivided into two storeys, the higher storey in each case being essentially an entresol (mezzanine) above a timber floor carried on corbels. The lower of the two stages is covered by a semi-circular barrel vault. The upper stage, which is very much taller than the lower, contains the tower's principal residential accommodation, and is covered by a pointed barrel vault which supports a stone-flagged roof. The walls are constructed of squared rubble, now covered with lime render, and rise without break into the parapet of the wall walk that runs around all four sides of the tower (Fig 19.1).

The ground floor now has its own entrance, though this is perhaps unlikely to reflect the original arrangements, and there are slit windows in three of its walls. The entresol floor above it has similar slit windows, but in this case they are in all four walls. It is not known what provision for access was initially made between the two lowest floors. The entresol can be reached by a narrow mural stair at the north-west corner, which descends from the hall on the floor above, and there may have been a trap door from the entresol to the basement. The hall, which is at the lower level of the upper stage, has the main entrance to the tower in its east wall, and there is evidence around the outside of the door for what is thought to have been the seating associated with a timber forestair and retractable bridge of some form. Within the hall there is a mural latrine closet at the north-east corner, a fireplace in the south wall, and an ogee-headed recess in both the north and south walls. Three staircases lead out of the hall. One, which has already been mentioned, descends to the entresol of the lower stage, and, very unusually, one rises to each of the two chambers within the upper vault, though one of those stairs appears to have been a later insertion. The two chambers at the top level were presumably originally separated by a timber partition resting on the floor joists; each of them has a fireplace, though only the eastern chamber has a latrine closet. The wall walk must have been reached by a timber ladder from the eastern of these chambers.

From at least the early 17th century the tower ceased to serve as a principal residence of the family that owned it, and over the past century it has been put to mainly agricultural uses, including that of a pig sty. Such uses, while not particularly dignified, did at least mean that it survived with very few changes, and it is known that some works were carried out to ensure its continued preservation in the early 1800s. The tower's historic and architectural significance was formally recognised in 1934, when it was scheduled as a

Figure 19.1 Liberton Tower

monument of national importance, and twenty years later its owners, the Liberton and Craigmillar Estate, offered it as a candidate for state guardianship. However, the anticipated stabilisation costs of up to £3400 were deemed to be prohibitive at that time. Following a further half century when little was done, in 1987 a body led by David Lumsden of Cushnie, which was then called the Historic Castles of Scotland and was later renamed the Castles of Scotland Preservation Trust, said it was considering restoring the castle as a museum. After further discussions with the owners, in 1992 the Trust took out a 100-year lease on the tower, and in the following year the architects Simpson and Brown drew up proposals for restoration. The work was eventually carried out between 1996 and 1998 under their supervision, with Ian Cumming as building contractor; there were further works in 1999. The work was supported by the Heritage Lottery Fund, and Historic Scotland allocated grant assistance of £189,200.

The initially intended use of the restored tower as a museum was eventually assessed as being financially impracticable. It was decided instead that the most appropriate use would be for letting as holiday accommodation, a use to which it has lent itself with great ease and with considerable acclaim by those who have stayed there. It is administered for that purpose by the Vivat Trust, which also administers Hallbar Tower, another of the case studies covered in this book. The basement, which has very low headroom, is used for storage and as a boiler room, and a modern concrete stair has been constructed to provide access down from the lower entresol. The lower entresol itself, which also has relatively limited headroom because of the curvature of the semi-circular vault, has been subdivided to house the kitchen and bathroom. The space that was the original hall of the house has been fitted out as the drawing room (Fig 19.2). A small dog-leg draught screen has been formed round the entrance and latrine closet which, although of clearly modern construction, may perpetuate the location and form of an original screen. Within the upper vault, over the hall, two bedrooms have been formed, with a lavatory within the latrine closet located above the one in the hall, which is drained by a pipe down the original chute. From the smaller of the two bedrooms a step ladder has been provided to give access to the wall walk. The interiors have been handsomely fitted out and furnished by the firm of Stuart Interiors (Fig 19.2).

Figure 19.2 Liberton Tower, the hall

The process of restoration at Liberton proved to be relatively straightforward, since it had survived in a largely complete state. As is so often the case, however, the biggest questions related to the treatment of the wall head and its parapet. The open wall walk at the wall head is finished with the usual arrangement of alternating runnels and saddle stones, and the wish to avoid disturbing these as far as possible has resulted in some difficulty in ensuring that the tower is fully water-tight. So far as the parapet is concerned, this was of the type that is found in a number of earlier towers, but also in some later towers of relatively simple construction. It was essentially an upward continuation of the wall faces of the main body of the tower, with no corbel table to project it outwards so as to gain extra width for the wall walk. The form of any crenellation to such parapets can vary greatly, and in the absence of clear evidence, it was decided that it would be least misleading for it to be simply finished off with horizontal coping (Fig 19.1). In order to ensure that the treatment adopted for the parapet would not confuse future investigators, the junction of the historic and new masonry was marked by a line of slates and, although this is now hidden by the external render of the masonry, it provides a clear record within the building to supplement that provided by the drawn and photographic records of the operation.

The reinstated external lime render of the masonry, which was based on analysis of a small number of surviving fragments, extends across the dressed masonry of doorways and windows, as is known to have been the almost invariable practice before the end of the 17th century. So far as the windows are concerned, in the upper parts of the principal openings there was clear evidence of the chases into which the glass itself was set, while within the embrasures were rebates for the frames to house two levels of shutters. The restoration of the windows was made more straightforward by the discovery of one of the quarries (small diamond-shaped panes), which permitted an accurate understanding of the form of the glazing to be reached.

CHAPTER 20

Melgund Castle

The estates and barony of North Melgund, Angus, were acquired by Cardinal David Beaton, Archbishop of St Andrews, in 1542 (Fig 1.15). He immediately set about transferring them to David, one of his sons, who would otherwise have been debarred from any inheritance on account of Beaton's own clerical status and his son's consequent illegitimacy. But the new castle he built was evidently intended from the start to be the principal residence of his mistress and the mother of his children, Marion Ogilvy, who was to live at Melgund until her death in 1575. There is no reason to doubt that building of the castle started immediately following acquisition of the estates, and the placement of the arms and initials of both Beaton and Ogilvy suggests that it was substantially complete by the time of Beaton's assassination in 1546.

The great interest of Melgund lies in the sophistication of its planning, at a time when domestic amenity had generally come to be accorded a greater priority than defensibility. As we have seen in many of the case studies in this book, since at least the 14th century the principal accommodation within aristocratic residences in Scotland had most commonly been in a tower-like structure; in these the rooms of the owner's lodging, consisting of a hall and one or more chambers, were stacked vertically above a vaulted basement. Such towers were almost invariably combined with a variety of other domestic and ancillary buildings set around the perimeter of one or more courtyards. As was outlined in the first chapter, however, and as is particularly clearly seen at Balgonie, by the later 15th century, if not before, it was becoming increasingly common for the owner's principal lodging to be planned as a horizontally arranged sequence of rooms that tended to have thinner walls and larger windows than in the tower. Such lodgings were usually elevated above a vaulted basement for reasons of prestige, security and insulation from dampness, with the basement rooms housing domestic functions and storage. The main accommodation within the lodging usually consisted of a hall and a chamber with associated closets, and there were cases where the immediately adjacent level within the tower appears to have been adapted to house the chamber. More often, the horizontally arranged lodging was occupied largely independently of the tower, even if it was physically attached to it, which presumably meant that in the new arrangements the tower was either expected to serve as a secondary lodging or as a series of separately occupiable chambers.

The particularly fascinating feature of Melgund is that it has a tower and a hall-and-chamber range combined within a single unified design (Fig 20.1). Although it has been speculated that the two parts could have been built

Figure 20.1 Melgund Castle

separately, close examination of the fabric and of the relationship between the parts suggests this is unlikely. So far as is now known, it is the earliest example of such a composite but chronologically homogeneous structure.

The tower house element of the castle, which has three main storeys and a garret above the two-compartment barrel-vaulted basement, is more thickly walled than the rest of the building, presumably because it rose to a greater height. Projecting from the eastern end of its north face is a substantial stair turret that straddles the junction with the rest of the building, and gives access to both parts (Fig 20.2). Extending back from the stair across the north face of the tower is a shallow projection that houses a corridor at basement level and closets above. The wall walk that runs around the top of the tower is projected out on a carefully detailed corbel table, and the skyline is further elaborated by a tall cap house rising over the stair that gives the tower a highly enriched silhouette (Fig 20.1).

The hall-and-chamber range extends eastwards from the tower, and its south wall is a continuation of that of the tower. Its basement consisted of five narrow barrel-vaulted bays, with the kitchen in the bay immediately next to the tower, where there was a large fireplace and bread oven. Running along the north side of

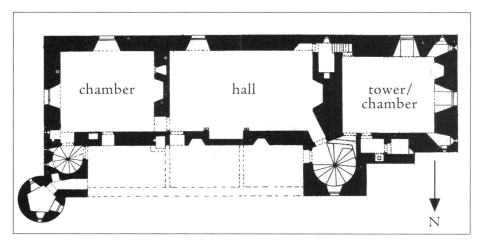

Figure 20.2 Melgund Castle, the plan (after MacGibbon and Ross)

this range, between the stair projection of the tower house element and a three-quarter-round tower at the north-east angle of the hall and chamber, was a relatively lightly constructed lean-to. The entrance vestibule and a corridor ran along the ground-floor level of this lean-to, and at first-floor level it contained a number of smaller rooms that may have functioned as closets to the principal lodging. Within the hall of this range there is little doubt that the high table was set at the eastern end (Fig 20.3), which was furthest away from the tower. The handsome fireplace is closer to that end, presumably because the western end was partly screened off as a vestibule and service area, and horizontal chases in the wall suggest there was a wainscot lining around the area of the high table. There was probably a buffet for the display of household plate on the wall opposite the fireplace, where two windows are set high in the wall.

The arrangements at Melgund suggest that there were two sets of principal chambers. One was at the west end of the hall, where the chamber beyond the high table end of the hall was supplemented by one or more smaller chambers or closets in the north lean-to, and also by a garret chamber above the main chamber. Interconnecting the ground floor with the two levels of this lodging was a stair at the eastern end of the lean-to, which permitted a high degree of privacy to the occupant of this lodging, as well as to any who might require to have discreet access to him. However, the vertically stacked chambers within the tower provided accommodation of a similar quality to that beyond the hall. Bearing in mind the somewhat irregular circumstances of the supposedly celibate cardinal's household, it may be that the provision of two such fine separate lodgings was an attempt to preserve at least something of the appearance of non-conjugal domesticity.

In all of this it is clear that the greatest care was taken to contrive arrangements that would permit a very high level of personal convenience and amenity for the principal individuals for whom Melgund was built. Nevertheless, there were also provisions for defensibility, as is evident from the array of wide-mouthed gunholes in the exposed north face, and in the north-east angle tower. The wish to have a residence that had at least some of the external trappings of a castle might certainly be a component of a newly emerging consciousness of the past that

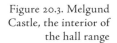

Figure 20.3. Melgund Castle, the interior of the hall range

found expression in the early Renaissance. This does not mean that defensibility was not taken seriously in the design of Melgund, and at a time of religious turmoil Beaton, as leader of the Church in Scotland, must have been acutely aware that he had many mortal enemies. Indeed, although his archiepiscopal castle at St Andrews had been formidably fortified with artillery blockhouses at each end of the entrance front during his uncle's episcopate, even that was not to be enough to save the cardinal from assassination within that castle in 1546. At Melgund the main residential element of the castle – the part that has survived – would have been the culminating focus of a sequence of enclosures, often referred to as 'yards'. These would have housed additional ranges of buildings and gardens, and would also have enhanced the wider setting of the main building and the sense of visual climax as one approached it. Those enclosures could also have afforded some additional measure of defensibility if required.

Over subsequent centuries, the estate of Melgund passed through various hands, until it was acquired by Sir Gilbert Elliot through his marriage in 1746 to Agnes, the daughter of Hugh Dalrymple-Murray-Kynynmund of Melgund. In 1813 their son, who had already been ennobled as Baron Minto in 1797, was created Earl of Minto, with a second title of Viscount Melgund, which gave the castle a particular significance for that family. Although the castle no longer had a residential role for its owners, hardly surprisingly they were coming to relish its qualities as a Romantic ruin, and they had it painted as such on at least one occasion.

By the mid-20th century the state of the castle was beginning to be a cause of concern: both the basement vaults and the outer wall of the lightly constructed north lean-to range had either collapsed or were threatening to do so. In 1969 the castle was offered as a candidate for state guardianship, though the financial constraints of the time meant that it was not possible for that offer to be accepted. By the 1970s, when increasing numbers of people were beginning to be attracted to the possibility of restoring a castle for their own occupation, Melgund came to the attention of two potential restorers, in 1976 and 1977. Apart from the sheer scale of what was required at such a relatively large castle, however, there was the difficulty of acquiring sufficient land around the castle either to provide access or to protect the castle's setting. Consequently, both of those proposals proved abortive. In 1981 a further potential purchaser went so far as to commission the architects Cunningham Jack Fisher Purdom to prepare designs for the castle's restoration, though that was taken no further.

In 1990 Historic Scotland was informed by the present owner, Mr Martyn Gregory, a London-based art dealer whose future wife's family had strong local connections, that he had purchased the castle from Lord Minto, together with 14 acres of land. Mr Gregory commissioned Benjamin Tindall Architects to carry out research into the castle as a prelude to commissioning proposals for its restoration. As part of this process, a resistivity survey to the north of the castle was undertaken by SUAT Ltd in 1990, and excavations were carried out by John Lewis of Scotia Archaeology between 1991 and 1996. Traces of an entrance courtyard and metalled access road were found on the north side, and evidence of another enclosure was identified to the east. Archaeological evidence was also found of what appears to have been a circular garden building of some kind between the castle and the burn to its south; there was no indication of that building's intended use, though one possibility is that it was a dovecote.

By the mid-1990s Mr Gregory was able to move forward with proposals for restoration drawn up by Benjamin Tindall Architects, and with Ian Cumming as contractor. A castle such as Melgund presents greater problems for its future occupants and their professional advisers than a tower house that stands in isolation, on account of the great scale of the accommodation that had been provided. Quite apart from the fact that few modern families now require so much space, the costs of restoring the whole castle would be prohibitive for all but the wealthiest owners. In this case it was decided to restore no more than the tower house part of the complex, together with the vaulted basement of the hall-and-chamber range, leaving the main floor of the latter as a stabilised but roofless shell. Mr and Mrs Gregory's drawing room and principal bedrooms would be formed within the upper floors of the tower, above service accommodation in the basement; the kitchen would be recreated within the vault below the west end of the hall, where it had always been, with a dining and living room in two other vaults. The remaining vaults would be used for storage.

For rather complex reasons the castle had never been scheduled as an ancient monument, though it was listed as a historic building. As a consequence, the local authority was the first point of contact for the necessary statutory processes, though Historic Scotland was closely consulted since it is listed at category A, and Historic Scotland was happy to support the work in a range of ways. As a first stage in the operations, the parts that were to be treated as a roofless shell were consolidated in 1996, with the wall heads protected by a 'soft topping' of turf. In view of the castle's outstanding importance, a grant of £43,500 was allocated by Historic Scotland towards this work, with a grant of £13,000 towards the continuing archaeology; there was to be a further grant of £900 towards the consolidation in 1996. Restoration of the parts that were to be lived in was carried out between 1998 and 2001, and grants towards this aspect of the work totalling over £426,000 were provided.

Despite the collapse of the vaults beneath the hall-and-chamber range, the loss of much of the outer wall of the lean-to that ran along the north side of that range, and the destruction of sections of the spiral stair that served the tower house, the main body of the tower was relatively well preserved, and it was possible to carry out its restoration with little resort to speculation. There was, for example, sufficient evidence to permit the reinstatement of historically appropriate glazing in the windows, with the glazing itself set into chases in the upper parts of the stone window surrounds, and with two levels of shutters on the inner plane (see Fig 11.2). A certain element of creative licence was introduced in the ceiling of the first-floor chamber within the tower, which was to be used as a drawing room. Here the joists were concealed above boarding, and a geometrical pattern of ribbing was applied to it that was based on the design of ceilings that have survived in the palaces of Holyrood and Linlithgow, and which are themselves roughly contemporary with Melgund.

Figure 20.4 Melgund Castle, work at the wall head (Martyn Gregory)

The greatest area of uncertainty was at the wall head (Fig 20.4). Parapets around the wall walks of 16th-century tower houses were usually crenellated and constructed of a single skin of ashlar that was structurally more vulnerable than the rest of the tower. Rather unexpectedly, at Melgund balusters were found in the course of excavation, and there was speculation that there could have been a balustraded parapet around the wall walk, though this was eventually concluded to have been unlikely in the mid-16th-century building campaign. Consideration was given to reinstating a plain parapet, in order to avoid making any misleading statements about the completeness of our understanding of this part of the castle. However, it was eventually decided that, since a building of the date and high quality of Melgund would almost certainly have had a crenellated parapet, not to reinstate the parapet to that form would be even more misleading than to give it a potentially modern appearance, particularly since its absence would detract from what had initially been one of the castle's most prominent features. It was therefore ultimately agreed that a crenellated parapet should be reinstated (Fig 20.1).

The course that was adopted at Melgund of restoring only one part, while leaving the rest as what might be described as a picturesque ruin, is in some ways unusual. It is certainly not uncommon for parts of a complex of buildings to be restored while others are left as ruins, and amongst the other cases of restoration described in this volume this has been done at Balgonie and to a lesser extent at Monimail. The difference at Melgund is that these two approaches have been adopted in the same building. Perhaps in some ways this is reminiscent of the Neoclassical Romanticism of the later 18th and earlier 19th centuries, when a number of houses were designed to have the external appearance of ruins. However, while it is not a course that is likely to be followed in a large number of other cases, it is certainly something that could be considered at comparable cases elsewhere.

CHAPTER 21

Hallbar Tower

Hallbar is a diminutive tower house situated on the picturesque wooded bank of the Braidwood Burn (formerly known as Fiddler's Burn), Lanarkshire (Fig 1.16). It is constructed of rubble masonry, and is set out to a square plan with sides of only 7.55m (Fig 21.1). There were two entrances: one into the basement, and the other at first-floor level. The latter appears to have been initially reached from the wall walk of a courtyard wall, and the jamb of a gateway through that wall survives below the upper doorway. Between the barrel-vaulted basement and an upper barrel vault there are three floors, and there is a garret within the roof. Access between the floors is by means of straight flights that wind around the four sides of the tower within the thickness of the walls. The only fireplace is at first-floor level, where the hall was presumably located, and there is also a small mural closet at that level. The owner's chamber was probably at second-floor level, where there is a corbelled-out latrine, albeit one that dates from the 19th century in its present form. The simple form of the tower, and especially the square plan and straight mural stairs, led early commentators to see it as being an early example of the type. However, it is in fact almost certainly of late 16th-century date and was probably built after the lands of the barony of Braidwood were granted to Harrie Stewart of Gogar in 1581.

The design of the wall head has a number of rather unusual features, though it is no longer clear how far these reflect the original arrangements, or to what extent they are creations of a major 19th-century restoration. The crow-stepped gables that contain the roof rise sheer above the lower walls. At the centre of one gable a small oriel is corbelled out, while the other gable has the nesting boxes of a dovecote, the main body of which appears to have been of timber and cantilevered out on beams from the wall face. On the two other sides crenellated parapets are corbelled out, at the end of one of which is a cap house with a pyramidal roof (Fig 21.2). It is only by way of the parapet wall walk that access is gained to the garret. The tower has had an associated barmkin of roughly triangular shape, which was 36m long by a maximum of 20m wide, and which occupies the plateau of a promontory formed by the confluence of two streams. Within the enclosure are the slight traces of other buildings.

The castle was heavily restored by D R Rankine in 1861, for its owner, Sir Norman Macdonald Lockhart, whose main residence was at Lee Castle. For several decades during the 20th century it was occupied by tenants, despite being designated as a scheduled monument as early as 1920. Indeed, in 1947 the architect Ian Lindsay drew up proposals for further restoration as an occasional retreat for the Revd Dr Nevile Davidson of Glasgow Cathedral,

who had taken a lease of the castle. It was later used for the meetings of the Carluke Parish Historical Society, though it was by then subject to increasing vandalism.

The tower was empty from 1984 until the Lee and Carnwath Estate approached The Vivat Trust fourteen years later, offering the trust a full-repairing lease on the tower. The project was taken forward with great enthusiasm by Francis Lloyd of the Vivat Trust, under the supervision of Peter Drummond and Jim Grant of A R P Lorimer Architects, and it was formally opened in May 2000. The project was funded by number of bodies, including the Heritage Lottery Fund and the Architectural Heritage Fund. Historic Scotland contributed around £127,700 to the project from its Historic Building Repair grant scheme.

In deciding what use would be most appropriate for the tower, it had been quickly concluded that a number of factors meant it would not readily lend itself to occupation by a modern family. These factors included the steep and narrow stairs and the limited range of accommodation, culminating in a top storey that could only be accessed from the parapet walk. There is also the complication that a right-of-way passes through the grounds of the castle. Taking account of these limitations, adaptation for self-catering holiday accommodation presented itself as an ideal solution. It also meant that a certain amount of public access could be maintained, which was an important consideration for a number of the funders.

Figure 21.1 Hallbar Tower

Figure 21.2 Hallbar Tower, a detail of the restored wall head

Although the building was structurally largely complete before the restoration project began, work on it was to present a number of significant challenges, requiring a high level of on-site supervision by the project team. When reroofed in the 1860s heavy stone flags had been employed. This was a distinctive feature of the castle, though by 1998 that roof was failing and it was clear that the overlapping stone slabs, which were pointed with mortar on both vertical and horizontal edges, would be difficult to make fully water-proof; they were also imposing a considerable extra weight on the roof timbers. After careful consideration it was therefore decided to replace the heavy stone flags with lighter slates, particularly since it was considered that slates were more likely to have been the material employed in the 16th century. Careful thought also had to be given to the best means of water-proofing the parapet walk, an area of a tower house that is always prone to the ingress of water. The fitting of a damp-proof membrane below the slabs of the wall walk would have required dismantling and rebuilding the parapet wall, and this would have been a major undertaking since it was still structurally complete. It was therefore decided that the joints of the saddles and troughs should be thoroughly tamped and pointed, and the situation is being monitored; so far this appears to have been a successful approach to dealing with the problem.

Figure 21.3 Hallbar Tower, the hall

The stairs also presented significant issues: some treads were damaged, while the individual steps were generally uneven and of differing tread depths. However, it was accepted that nothing should be done that might alter their historic character, and repairs were therefore restricted to a number of indents to the most damaged treads. Tensions inevitably arise in attempting to make tower houses safely accessible by modern standards, while not unacceptably modifying their character, and this was a particular problem at Hallbar. It eventually had to be conceded that there would be some visitors who would be unable to cope with climbing the stairs between the different levels of the tower, and it was decided that an alternative means of providing holiday accommodation for those with mobility difficulties would be the conversion of an outbuilding in the grounds of the castle.

Throughout the works, the project team worked closely with North Lanarkshire Building Standards on these issues and also on the question of fire safety. An innovative way of dealing with the problems of escape from the upper floors has been to have the garret denoted as a place of refuge in case of fire, since it is above a fire-proof vault. The former dovecote door can serve as a fire service ladder access point in case of emergency.

Despite the diminutive scale of the tower, through careful management it has been possible to contrive a surprisingly large amount of accommodation. The vaulted basement has been fitted out as a small kitchen and dining area. The space that was the original hall of the tower serves as the living room (Fig 21.3) and can be accessed from either the kitchen by way of the internal stair or from the external forestair and from there through a small lobby. The mural stair rises to the second floor where there would have been the principal chamber. At this level, however, the stair is no longer continuous, and to reach the next flight it is necessary to cross the chamber. On account of this, a corridor had to be created to provide access to that stair, and a second subdivision was introduced to accommodate the main bathroom of the tower. These subdivisions are the only significant modification of the spaces within the tower, though they are structurally fully reversible. The floor above, which is set with the upper vault, is fitted out as a bedroom, and there is a further bedroom within the garret. However, the latter can only be accessed by going out onto the parapet walk, which can make a night-time trip to the lavatory a rather breezy affair!

CHAPTER 22

Monimail, Cardinal Beaton's Tower

The tower at Monimail (Fife) formed part of one of the manor houses of the bishops – later the archbishops – of St Andrews (Fig 1.17). Despite the association with Cardinal David Beaton suggested by the widely used name, it is not recorded that he made any structural contribution to the complex, though he certainly stayed there on occasion. It is known that the lands had been held by the bishops of St Andrews from at least the early 13th century, and there was certainly a house on the site by the time of Bishop William Lamberton (1297–1328), though it is doubtful if anything that is now seen could be as early as that. However, there are references to works in the time of Archbishop James Beaton (1521–39), Cardinal Beaton's uncle and predecessor in the archdiocese of St Andrews, and it is very likely that parts of what remains could date from his episcopate.

The tower is the principal upstanding part of the residence, and as first built it was an addition to a range that ran along the south side of the principal courtyard; its arrangement of rooms may indicate that it initially functioned as a chamber tower to the north-east of that range. One window jamb and rear-arch springing of the south range is to be seen projecting from the south-west angle of the tower, and there are traces of another blocked window of that range in the wall that has been absorbed in the south face of the tower. The fact that one of the range's windows was blocked by the tower clearly shows that it pre-dated the construction of the tower, while the scale of those windows indicates that they lit a space of considerable size, and it is attractive to think that the space could have been the hall of the residence. Of the courtyard that extended to the north of the tower, what is probably the truncated end of the courtyard's east wall can be seen at the eastern end of the tower's north face. That wall must once have extended up to a small angle tower, the base of which was investigated in the course of excavations in 1987; that angle tower is probably datable to the mid-16th century on the evidence of its wide-mouthed shot-hole.

After the Reformation the estate was sold to Sir James Balfour in 1564, at which time it was said that the house was ruinous and could only be repaired at great cost. Major works were clearly carried out by Balfour, since the finely detailed parapet of the tower is dated 1578 and bears his arms and initials, while the polygonal cap house of the stair at the north-east corner is decorated with relief heads within roundels (Fig 22.1), reflecting a sculptural tradition seen previously in royal works of the 1530s at Falkland and Stirling Palaces. Balfour may also have built a forestair to a doorway at first-floor level of the tower, which is shown on early views, but which has since been removed.

In 1593, the estate was again sold, to Sir Robert Melville of Murdocairnie, who in 1616 was created Lord Melville of Monimail. His grandson, the first Earl of Melville, abandoned the remodelled episcopal manor house, replacing it with an imposing classical residence in the valley to its south, which was designed and built by the gentleman-architect James Smith in the years around 1700. Although the greater part of the old house was demolished, the tower was retained, presumably in order to provide an eye-catcher and place of resort within the landscape of the new house. It has subsequently been adapted on more than one occasion. Within the basement an octagonal vaulted ice house has been formed, while at ground-floor level three new openings were cut in the north wall to allow the tower to function in its newly isolated state. The chamber on the top floor was lined with timber (Fig 22.2), evidently in the early or mid-18th century on the evidence of the raised-and-fielded panelling and of the basket-arched fireplace. Gothick tracery that presumably dates from the later 18th or earlier 19th century has been inserted in the sash window in the south wall, from where it is possible to look across to the new house. The tower also now overlooks the immediately adjacent walled garden, which was built to its present form in 1825.

Figure 22.1 Monimail Tower

The tower was scheduled in 1937, when it was in the ownership of the Earl of Leven and Melville. Some 40 years later, when it was no longer part of that estate, an advisory report was prepared at the request of a new owner by one of the architects of Historic Scotland's predecessor body, at which time the external minor works were costed at £120. However, despite the relatively low anticipated costs, it did not prove possible for the owner to carry out those works at that time.

By the early 1980s, the tower had passed into the ownership of the Monimail Tower Project, a community whose main aims are horticultural and educational. That community took up residence within the walled garden, which was the principal focus of their activities, and in 1983 Historic Scotland's predecessors gave a grant of £600 towards excavation of the site of their new residential quarters by Kirkdale Archaeology. Further excavations by Middlesex Polytechnic in 1987 attempted to establish the relationship of the circular courtyard tower to the tower itself. By then it was becoming clear that remedial works would have to be carried out on the tower if its future were to be assured, and in 1991–92 the Monimail Tower Preservation Trust was set up for that purpose, taking out a ten-year lease on the tower in 1994. A condition report was prepared by Benjamin Tindall Architects in 1992, and the project was taken forward by the architect Tom Morton, who set about applying for grants from Historic Scotland and the

Figure 22.2 Monimail
Tower, the chamber
on the top floor

Heritage Lottery Fund for a full programme of works. It emerged at an early stage that an adequate understanding of the tower as a basis for undertaking its restoration could only be achieved if there were to be some archaeological investigation of its context. On that basis, between 1998 and 2001 grants totalling over £58,000 were awarded by Historic Scotland towards an archaeological watching brief and the consolidation of structures in the vicinity of the tower, including the stump of the angle tower of the courtyard that has been referred to above. Subsequently, between 2000 and 2003 Historic Scotland supported the writing up of the excavations by Stuart Farrell with grants of £6500.

In determining the way forward for the tower itself, for which the principal funding came from the Heritage Lottery Fund, the main considerations by the Trust were the tower's architectural needs and the provision of public access. On the latter point it was decided that the tower would be made freely available to visitors once work was completed, with some provision for a caretaker presence in a small flat that was to be created within a 19th-century offshoot of the tower. Consideration was also given to reopening a doorway into the basement of the tower, where the ice house is situated, but since this would have involved damage to the structure of the ice house the idea was soon abandoned.

So far as the architectural needs of the tower were concerned, several problems became apparent. The flat lead roof, which was leaking, was found on examination to be beyond repair, and was therefore entirely replaced. The windows and doors were also either in poor condition or entirely missing, and this had created problems of dampness and timber decay. As a result, one whole floor had to be replaced. So far as the walls were concerned, the masonry was badly decayed in several areas, and the chimney stack had to be rebuilt.

After the masonry had been consolidated by volunteer labour, with input from the Scottish Lime Centre, it was decided that the external render should be reinstated, based on analysis of surviving fragments. In carrying out this part of the work the main question was the extent of the new rendering. The approach eventually adopted was to apply the render only to those walls that had been externally exposed when the tower still formed part of the episcopal residence. For this reason the lower parts of the south wall, where it had abutted the adjacent range, and which embodied evidence for the fenestration of that range, were not re-rendered. Similarly the masonry was left exposed in the lower parts of the east end of the north face, since the truncated end of the courtyard wall survives at that point. The greatest difficulty was over the treatment of the wall-head parapet and stair cap house. Despite the fact that this was constructed of fine ashlar, it would almost certainly initially have been rendered or lime-washed in some way, and there was thus a case for reinstating that finish. However, there was insufficient evidence to do this with historic accuracy. This was a particularly significant consideration since the carved and heraldic detailing would have been tinctured and therefore particularly prominent, but no evidence had survived to show how that would have been executed. It also had to be borne in mind that repeated lime washing would have progressively obscured the fine detailing. It was therefore decided that the parapet and cap house should be left with their masonry exposed, though this decision can be revisited if further evidence comes to light (Fig 22.1).

Internally, once necessary repairs had been carried out on the plasterwork and woodwork, the main requirement was to carry out sympathetic redecoration. For the ground- and first-floor rooms, which had always been treated very simply, this was a relatively straightforward process, and once complete a small display on the history of Monimail Tower was introduced. The second-floor room had to be treated more sensitively, since, as has been said, its use as a prospect room by the occupants of Melville House meant that it was lined with panelling and heated by a handsome fireplace. Here the panelling has been painted a blue-grey colour based on paint analysis by Peter Hood, while the conservation of the stained glass in the south window was carried out by Trist and McBain. The designs of the new Delft tiles within the fireplace were based on those of a number of surviving damaged tiles (Fig 22.2).

The work on Monimail Tower has demonstrated how, if a project is properly managed, even a relatively impecunious Trust can achieve valuable results for historic properties in its ownership if it is able to attract sufficient grant assistance. However, there must often be a concern with such bodies that there is inadequate provision for ongoing maintenance, which may be exacerbated by lack of continuity in the personnel involved. Thus, while the Monimail Preservation Trust, which has recently been dissolved, certainly did succeed in its core mission of securing the tower's immediate future when it was at a critically vulnerable stage, there remains a requirement for long-term planning to take account of its ongoing needs.

Section Four
Conclusions

CHAPTER 23

The role of government in work on castles

In this penultimate chapter an attempt will be made to draw together some of the threads that have run through much of this book. This will take the form of a brief summary of the approach that is taken by Historic Scotland, on behalf of Scottish Ministers, in assessing proposals for works on castles or tower houses, and of the principles that underlie the advice that is likely to be offered on the way the work should be undertaken.

An outline has already been given in Chapter 3 of the legislative framework within which Historic Scotland operates, but beyond that framework account must also be taken of Scottish government policy on scheduled monuments and listed buildings. This is summarised in the *Scottish Historic Environment Policy*, which has been available online since October 2008, and which is periodically expanded and updated. The sections that are particularly relevant to work on scheduled monuments and listed buildings are currently at paragraphs 3.1 to 3.53.

In addition to the requirements of the legislation and the government's policy, valuable advice on the principles to be applied in works of this kind is to be found in a series of international conservation charters. The most directly relevant of these are the Venice Charter of 1964, and the Burra Charter as revised in 1999. Helpful guidance may also be found in the Charter for the Protection and Management of the Archaeological Heritage of 1990, while other charters have outlined the principles that should be applied in recording, and the principles for analysis, conservation and structural restoration of the architectural heritage. The latter were published in 1996 and 2003 respectively. Advice and guidance is also to be found in the British Standards Institute's *The principles of the conservation of historic buildings* of 1998.

When a decision has to be taken on whether or not a castle or tower house might be a suitable candidate for restoration, both its intrinsic importance and the proposed use have to be taken into account. At an early stage the question needs to be asked as to whether the cultural value of the castle could still be preserved for future generations if restoration to a structurally complete state were to take place. Conversely, it also needs to be asked if the cultural significance of the castle is so great that any works that went beyond the minimum necessary for long-term stabilisation would detract from that significance. In addition to those considerations, it is important to assess if the proposed new use for the castle could be accommodated within the existing fabric without the need for extensive alterations or additions that would damage its essential character.

Taking account of all of this, before any decision can be taken on whether or not a castle should be restored, it is important that a careful assessment of its cultural value and significance is undertaken by professionals who are qualified to carry out work of this kind. The most successful castle restoration projects are always based on a full understanding of the castles as buildings, and of the historical and cultural context within which they were created. It is therefore important that research is carried out into the documentation and other sources of information associated with the castles, in order to achieve that understanding. The assessments that are reached as a result of this work are often best presented within conservation plans. The conservation plans should also include sufficiently detailed preliminary surveys of the castle in its existing state, including measured drawings and photographs, so that the planning, architectural detailing and the inter-relationship between the parts are clearly recorded and presented, and fully understood.

Once these are in place, a start can be made on reaching an understanding of the castle's condition, in the light of its structural history, so that the measures which are likely to be required to place it in a stable condition over the medium to longer term can be determined by a properly qualified professional. That professional is likely to be an architect or engineer with experience in work of this kind, who can advise on the range of approaches that would result in conserving the fabric and protecting the cultural significance of the castle most effectively. Following on from that, a balanced evaluation of the relative merits of the possible approaches can be made, so that the one which would most appropriately meet the needs of the castle can be identified.

It should be accepted that, in the final analysis, there may be grounds for suggesting that restoration is not in the castle's best interests, especially at castles that are of altogether outstanding architectural, historical or archaeological value, and particularly where part of that value rests in features that are not to be found elsewhere. Restoration may also be considered inappropriate at castles that are particularly valued for their scenic qualities, that is, as what are sometimes referred to as 'ruins in the landscape'. This may especially be the case if a castle has been a significant source of artistic or literary inspiration as a ruin, or if it has particular resonances at a national or local level in its ruined state.

When restoration is agreed upon as an appropriate course of action, experience suggests it is likely to be most successful when the intended use is similar to the castle's original use, so that the design and layout can be most readily adapted to serve its new role. It is particularly important that the character of the castle should not be harmed by extensive modifications aimed at accommodating unsympathetic uses, by trying to fit too many functions into spaces that are inadequate for them, or by additions that are out of scale and character with the castle.

Proposals for restoration are also most likely to result in a successful outcome when the work can be carried out with a high degree of historic authenticity on the basis of the surviving architectural and archaeological evidence alone, or on the basis of a combination of that evidence and accurate pictorial evidence. As a starting point, there should usually be an assumption that all surviving historic fabric will be retained with as few changes as possible being made to it; it is also important to ensure that all new work could be removed if the need should arise without causing damage to that historic fabric. Here it should be borne in mind that some castles have been restored only to fall into ruin again at a later stage. Since restoration has not always proved to be a permanent solution to a castle's conservation needs, it should therefore be planned so that it will not make it more difficult for the historic fabric to survive any future changes of fortune.

There is almost invariably a need to renew or replace some missing details in the course of restoration, and this can pose a number of problems. Wherever possible, the design for replacement elements should be based on evidence within the fabric of the part of the building where the lost details were located. When this is not possible, a new element of sympathetic modern design is usually preferable to conjectural restoration, because details that might appear to be authentically historic but that are not in fact based on firm evidence may in future make it more difficult to understand the castle's architectural development. When new features have to be introduced, they should be tactfully distinguished from the original work, perhaps in one of the ways suggested in Chapter 11.

By planning the work in this way, the finished building will embody its own record of what has been done to a considerable extent, though it is still essential that detailed records should be kept of the work. In addition to any conservation plan, the initial survey drawings and the proposals and specification for restoration, together with drawn and photographic records of the state of the castle before, during and after restoration, should be carefully maintained. In due course copies of all of these should be deposited in the appropriate national and local archives.

When proposals for restoration are being prepared, it should be remembered that historic buildings are always more than just the sum of their individual component parts. They usually have a range of historical, cultural and emotional associations that give them significance for their local community and sometimes for the nation as a whole, and it is important that nothing is done that might detract from those qualities. Beyond that, since most historic structures are the product of more than one phase of construction, it is preferable if all of those phases are respected and the evidence for them retained in place. This means that, as a general rule, any process of restoration of a castle should see its most recent known state before abandonment as the end to be aimed for.

In exceptional circumstances, where restoration can be shown to be the most viable way of ensuring the long-term survival of a castle, but where there is insufficient evidence for this to be based in all respects on the castle's historic state, there may be a case for considering proposals that take the existing fabric as a starting point for a more architecturally creative approach to restoration. However, in such cases it would be essential that the historic fabric is itself retained with as few changes as possible, and it is preferable if the additions are fully sympathetic in their scale and use of materials. Those additions should also be identifiable as such.

A perennial problem in restoration projects is providing services such as water, drainage, electricity, gas and telecommunication connections without causing major disruption to both the upstanding fabric and the underlying archaeology. The most careful consideration is therefore required when deciding on service routes through and around the structure, and it is often sensible to use existing voids such as latrine chutes, or breaches in the masonry. All necessary ground disturbance should be carried out under the supervision of a team of experienced archaeologists, and it is important to include an adequate level of funding in the budget to meet not only the anticipated costs of the excavation, but also the post-excavation work and the eventual publication. All disturbance to the fabric should be supervised and recorded by archaeologists or architectural historians with experience in work of this kind, so that a full understanding can be reached of the evidence that is encountered, since in many cases that evidence can greatly enhance the understanding of the building.

Consideration should also be given to the impact that restoration might have on the wider archaeological, landscape and ecological context of the castle. Advice on this should be sought from the appropriate national and local bodies at an early stage of the process.

The most careful consideration should be applied to the design and location of any new buildings that might be considered necessary within the setting of a castle that is to be restored. It may be that, if extensive new buildings are likely to be needed, especially where such new buildings might be intrusive or out of scale, the castle is in fact not well suited to the applicant's particular needs, and an alternative should perhaps be sought. Where new buildings are to be provided, in some cases it may be appropriate to consider placing them on the footprint of destroyed buildings whose plans have been archaeologically investigated; but in such cases great care is required to ensure that the new buildings are of a scale and character that is related to that of the buildings on whose footprint they rest as well as of the restored castle itself.

In conclusion, however, it can be affirmed that, as many of the case studies covered in this book demonstrate, where restoration is agreed upon as the best way of securing a castle's future, and when all of the factors discussed above have been taken into account, restoring a castle – and living or working in that restored castle – can be a very rewarding experience.

CHAPTER 24

A retrospective
view

by Professor David Walker, sometime Chief Inspector of Historic Buildings

> '... we have endeavoured to fit the castle into what we pretend
> to be our necessities ... whereas we ought perhaps to proceed on
> the basis of fitting ourselves into the castle as she is with the very
> minimum of disturbance.'

So wrote the Hon. Clive Pearson to Sir Robert Lorimer in deciding against the schemes for the aggrandisement of Castle Fraser (Aberdeenshire) in 1922–27 (Fig 24.1). In Pearson's mind must have been Barra Castle (Aberdeenshire), where in 1910–11 the Aberdeen architect George Bennet Mitchell had retained its uniquely unspoiled atmosphere by accommodating the Irvines' requirements without any structural addition or alteration. He must also have been aware of Lorimer's own similar recovery of the original qualities of the derelict Earlshall (Fife) for his sensitive client, the bleacher R W R Mackenzie, at the outset of his career in 1891–94. Pearson's wording closely reflects the advice given by Historic Scotland and its predecessor departments to prospective castle restorers since at least the 1950s.

Some seventeen larger castles were reroofed and reoccupied as country houses between 1869 and the First World War, but, beyond continuing what had already been begun, none was undertaken in the inter-war years. The restoration of Scottish castles has been very much a post-war phenomenon, made possible by grant aid after the government set up the Historic Buildings Council for Scotland in 1953 to administer grants. The purpose of this retrospective is to set out the writer's experience of how the government's approach has evolved to meet the parallel challenges of a rising demand for such houses from a new generation of restoring purchasers and a fast-declining stock. Unlike the English manor houses built in the same years, the tall tower houses with tight turnpike stairs commissioned by Scotland's more security conscious landed gentry in the 15th, 16th and 17th centuries had not met the standards of comfort expected since the mid-18th century. By the late 19th century, many that had not been incorporated into larger houses were either roofless or falling out of use as farm servants' accommodation.

The first cases to come before the fledgling Historic Buildings Council were Pitheavlis (Perthshire) and Menstrie (Clackmannanshire) in 1954 and 1957. Both were conversions to municipal housing, with the compromises to the original

Figure 24.1 Castle Fraser (© National Trust for Scotland/ Ian Davidson)

planning that entailed, and they remain the only instances of their kind. The pattern for most post-war restorations was set at the dilapidated House of Aldie (Perthshire), planned by Ian Lindsay for Archibald Hope Dickson in 1938 on the lines set out in Pearson's letter. However, it was not acquired until 1947, was delayed by building licensing, and was only eventually completed with grant aid a decade later. Lindsay also set the precedent for the extraction of castles from Victorian additions at the Forbes house of Druminnor (Aberdeenshire), which Margaret Forbes-Sempill had bought back in a derelict state. This was an exercise repeated by the Aberdeen architect John Lamb at Udny (Aberdeenshire) for Margaret Udny-Hamilton in 1964–67, and again at Abergeldie (Aberdeenshire) for John Gordon in 1969–70.

All three of these were for the families which had originally built those houses and the repair element at Druminnor was happily accepted by both the Historic Buildings Council and the Minister in 1958. Lamb's proposed restoration for Mark Tennant of the dilapidated but still roofed Forbes tower house at Balfluig (Aberdeenshire), a smaller building but generally similar in architecture, brought about a serious confrontation between the council members and the then Minister of Public Buildings and Works, Charles Pannell, in 1965. The parallel application in respect of Hills (Kirkcudbrightshire) raised no problem, as it had a crenellated parapet and was recognisably a castle to English eyes, but Balfluig had tall pitched roofs and was not so recognisable. Not even the most trenchant writing by Dr W Douglas Simpson, as chairman of the Ancient Monuments Board, would change the Minister's mind. The issue was not resolved until July 1966, when the Secretary of State for Scotland became the Minister for both the Historic Buildings Council and the Ancient Monuments Division. A more sympathetic view could now be taken in respect of the Scots Renaissance tower houses, and gradually the Historic Buildings Council and its advisers – the late Stewart Cruden and Iain MacIvor – adopted a more adventurous course. The reluctant acceptance of the demolition of the fissured but still important mid-15th-century tower house at Elphinstone (Midlothian), the consolidation of which had been ruled out as unaffordable a few years earlier, had concentrated their minds. With some 60 castles already taken into care since the passing of the Ancient Monuments Act of 1900, and estates unwilling to spend large sums on structures of no beneficial use, it had become evident that wherever practicable other solutions would have to be found for most of the other major tower houses still at risk.

Thus in 1969–70 the sculptor Gerald Ogilvie Laing was given grant aid to restore the 1594 tower house at Kinkell (Ross-shire), then in a very similar state to Balfluig. A mid-18th-century wing was removed to clarify the original plan form and reduce the scale and cost of the works, a decision that might cause some heart searching now. Rather more significantly for the future, the St Andrews architect Roy Spence was given grant aid to reroof the much more ruined late 16th-century Balfour house at Pitcullo (Fife), a decision influenced by the fine quality of the detail at its entrance jamb. As at Kinkell, a later addition, here very badly built, was removed to make the project more manageable. It was a bold step at the time, but the principle of giving grant aid to reroof was not entirely new. As has been seen in this book, the American architect Robert L McNeil of Barra had, very exceptionally, been awarded grant aid to consolidate and reroof the island castle of his forebears at Kisimul (Barra) as early as 1958 (see Figs 12.1–12.3). Elsewhere, at the long-running restoration of Breachacha (Argyll), the MacLeans of Coll had met all their own costs since 1961, as had the new owner of Castle Stalker (Argyll) from 1965: both of these had begun as Ian Lindsay projects.

The precedent having been set, in 1973–75 another two roofless towers, Balgonie (Fife) (see Figs 16.1–16.3) and Rusco (Kirkcudbrightshire), were rerocfed, the later ranges attached to them being left as roofless shells. Both were supervised by William Murray Jack. Of these, Balgonie was for a new owner and is a case study in this book, while Rusco was bought back by Graham Carson, a descendant of the original builders. Of the further six dilapidated but still roofed castles given grant aid in those years, the work at Castle Menzies (Perthshire) (see Figs 15.1–15.3) was undertaken by a clan society and is another case study in this book, while Saddell (Argyll) was the first Scottish project of Sir John Smith's Landmark Trust, with Stewart Tod as architect.

Balgonie and Rusco had been relatively straightforward reroofings as both were simple rectangular towers with cap houses. However, with the Aberdeen architect

William Cowie's restoration of the tall Z-plan castle of Harthill (Aberdeenshire), built in 1601 for the Leiths and recently acquired by the Americans Mr and Mrs Steve Remp, grant aid moved into more complex and expensive territory. Harthill stood structurally complete to the chimney heads and even had its gatehouse, but establishing the geometry of its roofs and their interconnections was a new challenge, reflected in what were at the time relatively high costs. Still more demanding was Pitfichie (Aberdeenshire), another Z-plan house of slightly earlier vintage built for the Hurry family, for which Cowie was also architect, with an Aberdeen antique dealer as his client. As its back wall had collapsed in 1936, it might well have been refused a grant as being too far gone, but the fallen masonry was still on site, the whole had been thoroughly recorded before the collapse, and Dr Simpson had thought highly of it. The Historic Buildings Council thus made the brave decision to support it. In doing so the council and its advisers had in mind John Lamb's very successful rebuilding of the partly fallen Inchdrewer (Banffshire) for Robin de la Lanne Mirrlees, a descendant of the original Ogilvie owners, which was undertaken without grant aid on the basis of archaeological evidence in the mid-1960s. At Inchdrewer the rebuilding had been in carefully matched rubble, but at Pitfichie blockwork was used, the result being surprisingly convincing as the original dressings were retrieved and reused as far as possible. Blockwork was also adopted at Ian Begg's 1978–85 rebuilding of the small tower house at Muckrach (Inverness-shire), built for the Grants of Rothiemurchus in 1598; this was more for speed of consolidation than cost, as it was badly holed and heavy timber had been used as reinforcement in the original masonry construction.

No less ambitious than Pitfichie was the engineer Tom Craig's rebuilding of Fawside (East Lothian), a 15th-century tower to which a 16th-century stepped L-plan tower had been added, both phases for the family of that name. Both parts had crumbled at the wall heads, which were rebuilt in brick, although the difference in materials below the harl became obvious in wet weather. More manageable in scale than either of these was the 1585 L-plan tower house of the Cairncross family at Hillslap (Roxburghshire), rebuilt by the architect Philip Mercer for himself. Here, after the tower itself was reconstructed in 1979–80, the rebuilding of the barmkin, gateway and kitchen wing followed in 1982–95, all on the basis of the archaeological evidence and original masonry found on site.

There were several major projects in the years 1977–80. At the 1577 Z-plan house of the Ogilvies at Carnousie (Banffshire), the local authority and the Historic Buildings Council had to accept the demolition of William Adam's derelict 1740 wing, the loss of Adam's fine interiors being still a painful memory for the present writer. Ian Begg and Lawrence Rolland heroically rescued Rossend (Fife) as their offices (see Figs 17.1–17.5), perhaps the most riveting case study in this book. The rehabilitation for Rick Wharton in 1977–80 of the great Gordon house of Midmar (Aberdeenshire), built by George Bell in the 1570s and enlarged in 1733, resolved a long-standing anxiety as it had been empty since 1842.

Inevitably, all these major cases were expensive, and the combination of rapid inflation in building prices – 27% in 1977–78 alone – and a changeover in 1979 to cash limits on the Historic Buildings Council's actual payments, rather than on the allocation of grants, caused overwhelming problems for the Council, to which the writer had become assessor following the transfer in 1978 of the Ancient Monuments service from the Property Services Agency of the Department of the Environment to the Scottish Office's Historic Buildings Branch, these now forming the Historic Buildings and Monuments Division. Continuing expenditure on Pitfichie and Fawside was particularly heavy, and in 1981 the Council ordered a review of expenditure on castles and on possible future commitments, which was undertaken by the writer with the help of Rebecca Barker, the grants in previous years being recalculated to 1981's values. This showed that the Council's expenditure on castles had doubled from about 7.5% to 15% of total expenditure. The Council's chairman, the Earl of Crawford and Balcarres, concluded that the resources devoted to castle restoration had not been excessive, but confronted with a temporary moratorium on grant offers while all current applications were reassessed, the Council resolved to tighten the criteria for future cases.

Tillycairn (Aberdeenshire), a tall late 16th-century L-plan tower reroofed for David Lumsden, a descendant of the original builder, met the new criteria easily enough when it was considered in 1981, even if there was some doubt as to how the 17th-century alteration to the parapets flanking the stair head had been intended to be completed. But Castle Leslie (Aberdeenshire) and the part-restoration/part-consolidation of Roslin Castle (Midlothian) (see Fig 2.15) were to test the Council's new resolve. Leslie, built in 1661 for William Forbes of Monymusk whose father had acquired the estate from the Leslies, represented an important stage in the transition from tower house to restoration country house. The willingness of a descendant of the original owners, the architect David Leslie, to meet the greater part of the cost of retrieving it from complete collapse seemed too good a solution to be missed. The work at Roslin, one of the most romantic of all Scottish castle sites, and all the more important for its relationship to Roslin Chapel, was entrusted to James Simpson by the Earl of Rosslyn, with the Landmark Trust as end user.

Leslie was rebuilt in stone at £700 per square metre, but in the later stages, particularly at the missing top of the stair tower, economies had to be made. Roslin was completed to a consistently high standard, but costs increased. As a result of the new criteria and the economic difficulties from the later 1970s, there were only a few new cases in 1982–85. The Gordon house at Terpersie (Aberdeenshire), generally seen as the pioneer (1561) Z-plan house, was rebuilt by William Cowie for Lachlan Rhodes in 1983–89; Nisbet (Berwickshire) was a long-derelict house of c 1610 with important 18th-century interior work; and Methven (Perthshire), a towered square-plan house now known to have been built by James Smith for Patrick Smyth in 1678–82, was rescued from dereliction by the architect Ken Murdoch. Work on two important 15th-century towers was also undertaken. Law (Ayrshire) at West Kilbride was reroofed by Ian Begg for Dr Anthony Philips, and Niddry Castle (West Lothian) was reroofed by William Cadell for Peter Wright. The heavy commitment on these, coupled with further demands for supplementary grants on old cases as a result of continuing inflation of 23% since 1981, provoked a second review during a much more serious moratorium on new grant cases in 1985. Among the recommendations was a greater emphasis on conservation than on restoration, as has been seen in Section Two of this book.

The moratorium of 1985 lasted some sixteen months, with a working party chaired by the Marquess of Bute to sift applications and make recommendations on those applications which might in time be allowed to proceed. Difficult decisions were forced on the Council, and grant aid had to be refused at Blackhall (Renfrewshire) in Paisley, at Castle Levan (Renfrewshire) and at the Landmark Trust's Old Place of Monreath (Wigtownshire). In all three cases work nevertheless went ahead. Stephen Yorke's reroofing of Spedlins (Dumfriesshire), a 15th-century tower with a very sophisticated double-pile superstructure of 1605 built by the Jardines of Applegarth, was carried out in 1988–89 without any application for grant. Perhaps the most surprising by-product of the difficult economic conditions of the early 1980s was the Graham house of 1562 at Mains of Fintry (Dundee), restored by Dundee District Council with labour provided by the Manpower Services Commission, in fulfilment of that Council's legal obligation to keep the castle in good repair.

When grant-aided restoration of castles resumed in 1987–88, standards were consistently higher than they had been, and there were now specialist contractors skilled in building rubble masonry. There were several reroofing projects in those years. Work on the Oliphant family's Z-plan house at Hatton (Angus) was planned in 1985 but not executed until 1987–88, under the supervision of Douglas Forrest and in the day-to-day care of Ian Cumming. Midhope (West Lothian) was consolidated and reroofed by Willam Cadell for Hopetoun Estates in 1988–94. Carrick (Argyll) was reroofed by Ian Begg in 1988, and Forter (Angus) was reconstructed in 1989–92 by Nicholas Groves-Raines, old photographs helping with the reinstatement of fallen masonry. Groves-Raines subsequently undertook the similarly planned but rather larger Fenton Tower. At Aikwood (Selkirkshire), restored by Cadell and Malcolm Hammond for Lord and Lady Steel, and a case study in this book (see Figs 18.1–18.2), and at Tilquhillie (Kincardineshire), a major Z-plan house of 1576 rehabilitated by France Smoor Architects for Dr John Coyne, the original roofs were still in place and the work required was less radical. Those years were also remarkable for two major local authority restorations. The giant 15th-century tower of the Earls of Mar at Alloa (Clackmannanshire) was undertaken as a museum project by Clackmannan District Council's Alloa Tower Preservation Trust in 1989–96, with Bob Heath and Martin Hadlington as architects. Dundee District Council's great L-plan castle of Dudhope (Dundee) was reconstructed as offices in 1988, in a pragmatic compromise between Ian Lindsay's 1961 scheme for complete reconstruction to its late 17th-century form and its final state as adapted for barrack use in 1799.

Much has happened since the writer left Historic Scotland in 1993, as has been seen in the chapters on Liberton (Midlothian), Hallbar (Lanarkshire) and Melgund (Angus) (see Figs 19.1–19.2; 21.1–21.3; 20.1–20.4). There have also been major rebuildings at Ballone (Ross-shire), Stoneypath (East Lothian) and

Ballencrieff (East Lothian), the two last being more ambitious in what had to be done than at any others in the recent past. Awarding grant aid for the reroofing of castles has always had its critics, with the seemingly uncontentious restoration of the very complete Kirkhope (Selkirkshire) being opposed by a member of the Historic Buildings Council as late as 1993. The restoration of Forter, widely deemed to have been highly successful, was the subject of criticism at the Architectural Heritage Society of Scotland's Castle Culture conference as recently as April 2008. With the benefit of hindsight, a few might have been better consolidated, had the owners been willing to follow that route, and some could have been done better in other respects.

Until the mid-1960s it had seemed inevitable that a very high proportion of the finest Scottish houses of the 15th, 16th and 17th centuries would be lost. The 70-odd restorations undertaken since then which can be regarded as successful match in numbers, if not always in scale, those held in the guardianship or ownership of the state. They enrich the Scottish countryside and the frequent absence of later interventions has its merits in that long unoccupied houses can better illustrate how such houses were first designed to be lived in than continuously occupied ones. A great deal has been achieved by means of restoration for a relatively modest expenditure of public funds, and, although there is reduced scope for further projects, hopefully more will yet be achieved.

Suggestions for further reading

Legislation, policy, guidance and charters

Ancient Monuments and Archaeological Areas Act 1979

Ashurst, John, *Conservation of ruins*, Oxford, 2007

British Standards Institution, *The principles of the conservation of historic buildings*, London, 1998

Burra Charter, The Australia ICOMOS charter for places of cultural significance, 1979, revised 1999

Charter for the protection and management of the archaeological heritage, 1990

Dallas, Ross (ed), *Measured survey and building recording for historic buildings and structures*, Historic Scotland Guide for Practitioners, Edinburgh, 2003

GBG (GB Geotechnics), *Non-destructive investigation of standing structures*, Historic Scotland Technical Advice Note, Edinburgh, 2001

Historic Scotland, *The repair of historic buildings in Scotland*, Edinburgh, 1995

Historic Scotland, *The conservation of architectural ancient monuments in Scotland, guidance on principles*, Edinburgh 2001

Hughes, John J, and Válek, Jan, *Mortars in historic buildings*, Historic Scotland Literature Review, Edinburgh, 2003

Planning (Listed buildings and conservation areas) (Scotland) Act 1997

Scottish Historic Environment Policy (published online)

Scottish Lime Centre, *Preparation and use of lime mortars*, Historic Scotland Technical Advice Note, Edinburgh, 2003

Scottish Lime Centre, *External lime coatings on traditional buildings*, Historic Scotland Technical Advice Note, Edinburgh, 2001

Simpson and Brown, Architects, *Conservation of plasterwork*, Historic Scotland Technical Advice Note, Edinburgh, 1994

Urquhart, Dennis (ed), *Conversion of traditional buildings, application of the Scottish Building Standards*, Historic Scotland Guide for Practitioners, Edinburgh, 2007

Venice Charter, International charter for the conservation and restoration of monuments and sites, 1964

The castles

Billings, Robert William, *The baronial and ecclesiastical antiquities of Scotland*, 4 vols, London, 1845–52

Buildings of Scotland, Harmondsworth, London or New Haven and London, 1978–

Cruden, Stewart, *The Scottish castle*, Edinburgh and London, revised edn, 1963

MacGibbon, David, and Ross, Thomas, *The castellated and domestic architecture of Scotland*, 5 vols, Edinburgh, 1888–92

Maxwell-Irving, Alastair M, *The Border towers of Scotland … the West March*, Dumfries, 2000

McKean, Charles, *The Scottish chateau*, Stroud, 2001

Miket, Roger, and Roberts, David L, *The medieval castles of Skye and Lochalsh*, Portree, 1990

Oram, Richard, and Stell, Geoffrey (eds), *Lordship and architecture in medieval and Renaissance Scotland*, Edinburgh, 2005

Royal Commission on the Ancient and Historical monuments of Scotland, *Inventories*, Edinburgh, 1909–

Tabraham, Chris, *Scotland's castles*, London, 1997

Tranter, Nigel, *The fortified house in Scotland*, 5 vols, revised edn, Edinburgh, 1986

The cultural background

Andrews, Malcolm, *The search for the Picturesque*, Stanford, 1989

Davis, Michael C, *Scots Baronial, mansions and castle restorations in the west of Scotland*, Ardrishaig, 1996

Gilpin, William, *Observations, relative to Picturesque beauty, made in the year 1776, on several parts of Great Britain; particularly in the High-Lands of Scotland*, 2 vols, London, 1789

Grose, Francis, *The antiquities of Scotland*, 2 vols, London, 1789–91

Holloway, James, and Errington, Lindsay, *The discovery of Scotland* (National Gallery of Scotland exhibition catalogue), Edinburgh, 1978

Jokilehto, Jukka, *A history of architectural conservation*, Oxford, 1999

Macaulay, James, *The Gothic revival 1745–1845*, Glasgow and London, 1975

Pennant, Thomas, *A tour in Scotland MDCCLXIX*, Warrington, 1772

Pennant, Thomas, *A tour in Scotland and voyage to the Hebrides MDCCLXXII*, Chester, 1774

Restoration projects

Clow, Robert (ed), *Restoring Scotland's castles*, Glasgow, 2000

Fawcett, Richard (ed), *Stirling Castle, the restoration of the great hall*, Council for British Archaeology Research Report 130, York, 2001

Macneil of Barra, *Castle in the sea*, London and Glasgow, 1964

Stell, Geoffrey, 'Ruin, romance and revival: Scottish castles in the 19th century', in *Reconstruction or new construction of medieval castles in the 19th century*, Europa Nostra Scientific Bulletin, vol. 61, 2006

Excavation reports

Farrell, Stuart (ed), 'Monimail Tower: its history, architecture and archaeological investigations 1983–2000', *Tayside and Fife Archaeological Journal*, vol. 14, 2008, 69–98

Lewis, John, 'Excavations at Melgund Castle, Angus, 1990–96' *Tayside and Fife Archaeological Journal*, vol. 10, 2004, 135–52

Will, R S, and Dixon, T N, 'Excavations at Balgonie Castle, Markinch, Fife', *Proceedings of the Society of Antiquaries of Scotland*, vol. 125, 1995, 1109–18

Index